Retail Fashion Merchandise Planning and Trading

by

Charles Nesbitt

Copyright ©2016 by Charles Nesbitt. All rights reserved.

Copyright and ISBN page

Also by Charles Nesbitt

FUNDAMENTALS FOR SUCCESSFUL AND SUSTAINABLE FASHION BUYING AND MERCHANDISING

*

FUNDAMENTALS FOR FASHION RETAIL STRATEGY PLANNING AND IMPLEMENTATION

*

FUNDAMENTALS FOR FASHION RETAIL ARITHMETIC, ASSORTMENT PLANNING AND TRADING

*

THE COMPLETE JOURNAL OF FASHION RETAIL BUYING AND MERCHANDISING

*

RETAIL FASHION ARITHMETIC

*

RETAIL FASHION PROCUREMENT TEAM ROLES AND PROCESSES

Table of Contents

PREFACE 5
INTRODUCTION 6
   Retailing 6
   The retail players 6
THE PROCUREMENT TEAM 6
   Designers 7
   Buyers 8
   Merchandisers 10
   Technology 13
PROCESS FLOW OF KEY RETAIL ACTIVITIES 15
BUYING GROUP ORGANISATION 16
MERCHANDISE PLANNING 18
   Basic steps of planning process 21
      Plan markdowns 22
      Confirm opening stock 24
      Plan forward cover targets 24
      Derive closing stock values 25
      Determine the intake required 25
   Monthly financial planning 26
   Integration of hierarchy level plans 28
   Location plans 29
   The eighty twenty rule 31
   Sophisticated merchandise planning applications 31
MERCHANDISE ASSORTMENT PLANNING 32
   Department line sales summary 36
   Building the range plan 37
   Volume and choice balance 44
   Style and shape proportions 46

    Pricing structure 47

    Colour range 48

    Size architecture 49

    The use of trials 53

    Range presentations 53

    Store range profiling 56

STOCK MANAGEMENT 58

    Supplier meetings 60

    Negotiating 60

    Costings 62

ORDERING 65

PRODUCT ALLOCATION 69

REVIEW AND ACTION OPTIONS OF IN SEASON TRADING 73

    Process of comparing the actual performance in relation to the plan 73

    Analysis options 76

    Action options 78

POST SEASON TRADE ANALYSIS 79

    Product 79

    Customers and competitors 79

    Key performance Indicators 79

    Suppliers 80

    Stores 80

    Marketing 80

CONCLUSION 80

PREFACE

The process of buying and selling in some form or other of goods has been with us since time immemorial. Often when one stands in bewilderment in an elegant shopping mall and wonder how all the stores are able to effectively seduce the many shoppers trawling the wide corridors to readily part with their well-earned money while at the same time enabling them to possibly enjoy a wonderful social experience.

The plan of offering goods to the potential customer is a complicated one and is a science that involves many players whose individual contributions slot seamlessly together and are so perfectly coordinated that it provides the perception that it is the result of one individual concerted effort.

It will be illustrated as to how the relationships of the major functions that intertwine from the conceptualisation of a product through to the presentation of a finished garment to the potential customer and in doing this demonstrates how the key areas such as buying, merchandising, technology, production, design, logistics and selling each with their unique specialised operations manage to achieve this.

The book endeavours to try and outline the basic key principles and mechanisms by which this happens and should be helpful to students, people in retailing and those who are maybe considering a career in the industry. For those who already are part of the fashion buying and merchandising community this book will be beneficial in that it provides a complete simplified overview of all the integral activities and roles that go to make up the topic and thereby will provide a broader insight into their own career.

The material of the book, other than that specifically referenced is the result of the author's own exposure to the subject during a career spanning thirty five years at a major retail organisation in Southern Africa, the support from colleagues, mentors, interaction with suppliers and own research. There has been some cross referencing to other books or technical material but the book focuses largely at a higher level on the key principles, concepts and theories and hence there is none or very little mention of retailers by name or technological packages for some key activities such as planning, allocating, critical path management, logistics and the like.

The fundamental purpose is therefore to provide the basic background that goes into the operational and technical aspects which can be universally applied. While there is merit and great benefits in the use of sophisticated technical packages that live off a common database and also integrate with one another, sadly often the prime emphasis becomes more one of mastering the system and promotes the tendency to live in a silo environment. As a result the importance tends to be focused on that single facet that the system serves rather than the broader picture. The fact that there is a relatively limited amount of material that generally describes the practice commonly known as retailing as an end to end process considering the enormous size of the industry is one of the motivating reasons for the documentation of this book.

INTRODUCTION

Retailing

Retailing is the offer of goods or services for sale by individuals or businesses to an end user. The channels by which these goods reach the final user may vary considerably and arrive via different sources such as wholesalers, trading houses or directly from the manufacturer and there are equally many differing variants in the way the goods are put on sale. Historically it is more likely that shopping would have been done at the village or town market, in a high street shop or at the "mom and pop" store which evolved over time into mass retailing stores that are often housed in shopping malls supported by smaller line shops.

More recently with the advent of the computer utilising various platforms such as the internet or social networks, shopping on line is growing exponentially using electronic payment methods with delivery via the post or with a courier man knocking on the front door of the customer bearing their purchase relatively shortly after the transaction has been processed.

The products that are put on offer will be determined by the demand to satisfy a need in the market place. Broadly the merchandise may be categorized into food stuffs, hard or durable goods such as appliances, furniture and electronics and soft goods that have a limited life span typically clothing, apparel and fabrics. Whatever the nature of the product, the key objective will be to acquire and sell the product at a price that will be more than it cost to bring it to the place of offer and thereby make a profit. Supporting activities such as the storage, movement of the goods, technology, and marketing will endeavour to ensure that the form, function and profit objective is maximised.

The retail players

The saying "no man is an island" holds true in many spheres and this is certainly the case in the world of clothing retailing.

Various players, each with very different specialised skills are amalgamated together to deliver a completed outcome which is that of presenting product for sale to potential customers. These players are often very diverse not only in the activities that they perform but also in their personality traits which they possess. The key to a successful team is how maturely the interaction takes place and the mutual respect that every member has for each other's roles.

Below is a brief synopsis of the main player's roles and their dependency and integration with each other. The intimate details of the roles will be exposed in the future chapters as the science of retailing is explored in greater detail.

THE PROCUREMENT TEAM

The foremost players in the clothing and apparel procurement team consist typically of the following members and are described in broad terms.

Designers

Designers have a deep insight into the market they are targeting through the analysis of the changing trends and use these to provide creative direction and develop product designs for the buying teams to consider.

Usually these participants tend to think out of the box and their creative minds can challenge some of the comfort zones of other team members. What must be kept top of mind is that they need to consistently apply their intellect way ahead of time as to what they think the customer requires as opposed to their personal desires.

Typically the character traits which they will possess are that they are independent, spontaneous, extroverts, driven by ideas and are confident by nature.

Although the general perception of the word "designer" conjures up a vision of those who work at couture level, the reality is that it also includes those who are involved in creating ranges which may also be exclusive but will be more widely available and therefore can be considered as having been mass produced. Their choices will be influenced by the type of retailer they work for or the product category that they design for. The more traditional retailer which serves predominantly mature customers will be less influenced by radical fashion swings which in contrast will definitely affect the younger market's high fashion boutiques more rigorously.

Work is done at times under enormous pressure to meet critical deadlines, tough meeting schedules and involves frequent international travel. It is not surprising the perception is often one that they live a life of glory and glamour but contrary to this belief the reality is that it is not as extravagant as made out to be.

The fashion and trade shows, whether they be for yarn, fabric or garments are tiring affairs requiring hard work and stamina as is the shopping for appropriate samples, researching fashion magazines, the use of forecasting trend agencies, internet and blogs and out of all of this they need to possess the ability to then distil the emerging trends to create a storybook that will best suit their organisation's customer profiles.

The designer lives with the constant strain of knowing that their level of success will be measured by the eventual amount of money rung up at the till and getting the styling direction wrong or overextending the life of a particular look could have severe financial implications, especially in the cases where volumes are high.

The real challenge is to convince the buying teams and senior management to buy into their vision and have the confidence that what they have in mind will be commercially acceptable to the customer. The designer cannot ignore the technical aspects of the garment production as many problems can be evaded if these are taken cognisance of during the design process.

Retailers in the southern hemisphere do have the advantage that their seasons follow those of countries in the northern hemisphere which allows them to tap into the more successful designs that are trading in volume. However, with globalisation this is not always as clear cut as it was in previous years and the ability to follow as close to the season as possible requires techniques that facilitates the shortening of lead times and attempt to get the product to market as quickly as possible. The advent of communication technologies such as satellite television, internet and social media have brought exposure to different cultures, sports, films, lifestyles and trends such as those generated by specific events, health drives, environmental awareness and technology platforms that can have significant impacts on fashion which sometimes happen at very short notice.

A very important aspect is that the designer must adhere strictly to, is that of copyright. Instances have occurred that other competitor's garments are copied almost identically whether it be by style, print or design. Invariably the driving reason for this is the speed of being able to turn on a replica at a cheaper price. Although it may not be practical to register and copyright every design, any infringement can still be challenged and a consequence could occur of having the offending garments being removed from display and destroyed.

Buyers
The buyer needs to have a clear understanding of the product that is required which is in line with the trend guidelines best suited to their target customer profiles, for both the high fashion segment as well as those that best serve the more traditional customer.

It is a fact is that the role of the designer and the buyer may be a bit blurred in that they research the same fashion forecasting sites and other sources of inspiration in order to put a range of garments together. Both roles must be aware of sizing, quality and costs related to fabrics, trimmings and production. To achieve this successfully they must be flexible enough to develop and buy the most suitable product that is in line with the prescribed strategy and achieves the desired profit margin in keeping with the set down targets. The evaluation of competitive activity and product ranges through regular store visits and comparative shopping provides the knowledge required to keep ahead of the field.

Effective communication and presentation skills are a prerequisite to brief and interact with suppliers as well as presenting product reviews to colleagues within their own group at all levels of seniority. With this comes the need to be able to accept criticism and resolve problems in a mature manner. The sad fact is that frequently when the analysis of the success of the range is evaluated at the end of the season, if the results are disappointing it is not uncommon for the buyer to shoulder the emotional burden of the poor performance. The truth of the matter is that the range was presented on more than one occasion to all team players including senior management all of whom signed the range off but in the final analysis they are more often than not, as is human nature, reluctant to be accept any proper accountability.

Coupled to ability to understand the wants of the customer is the sourcing of the most suitable supplier that will be selected for the specified product types in terms of their particular skills, technical ability, costing efficiency, attitude, transparency, honesty, focus on quality, communications and competitiveness while still meeting the ethical criteria that are acceptable to society.

A large part of the task will be to maintain good relations with suppliers, while at the same time being able to assertively negotiate prices with them and make sure the planned stocks are delivered on time. Communications need to be clear and specific to avoid disputes over issues which may arise through vague and confusing messages. For these reasons they need to be confident, take decisions based on results and be driven by a sense of urgency.

The buyer has to be multi-talented in that as well as being creative they also need to monitor the sales objectively and be flexible enough to react accordingly in terms of turning on or turning off production and transferring fabric and components to more appealing product styles where sales performance and fast emerging trends dictate.

What is key to be a successful buyer is the ability to work as part of the overall team and influence the rest of the team's activities which could be in the form of a managerial and developmental capacity that could also include both their peers and superiors.

The display of emotional maturity and commercial acumen within the controlled parameters as set by the merchandising arm in terms of the budgets, the number of product options and display space constraints is absolutely essential.

The same principle applies to the relationships that need to be maintained with the technical teams in regard to the use of the most appropriate fabrics which meet the product form and function demands in addition to ensuring that the brand standards of the garment are observed.

The fact that potentially the buyer together with the other retail players will be dealing with three to four seasons simultaneously at different stages for each season makes their task even more complicated. To clarify the phenomenon a bit further, the journey of this book attempts to describe the process from beginning to end for one season but while trading in the current season the thoughts and strategies are being developed and documented for two or possibly three seasons ahead followed by the range development leading up to the production taking place for next upcoming season.

The ability to absorb and interpret vast amounts of information from various sources, much of which originates from complex IT systems, can present a challenge to those who are not analytically minded. Systems have altered the scope of the traditional buyer from being a pure "touchy feely art skill" to having to develop basic technical abilities through the continual emergence of innovative systems which have become a great advantage to the role.

Some buyer's, such as those for knitwear, ladies structured underwear, tailoring and footwear will require more expert fabric and garment construction knowledge of their respective industries in comparison to individuals who select the more straightforward cut, make and trim products such as dresses, blouses and casual trousers.

As the trade environment has become more global and through information technology development it is much faster, interactive and has enabled business to be done more effortlessly from a home base interacting with many different countries. A great deal of the job is done amongst many new emerging countries which has led to a need for urgency and nimbleness in order to locate the most effective plants that meet the quality requirements, be able to assess the required technical abilities, understand the economic and cultural demands of the respective countries as well as the logistical peculiarities and government regulations that may exist.

The sourcing of production has to take on different approaches as the pros and cons of dealing internationally needs to be carefully weighed up against those of dealing with the ever diminishing number of local suppliers. A critical factor is that suppliers must be ethical in terms of labour practices, remuneration, waste management, working conditions and safety. If such conditions are not met it is counter to the interests of the retailer to be associated with such suppliers from both a moral point of view and the exposure of malpractices could lead to negative media reports and the retailer will suffer the consequences that accompany such deeds. The measurement of performance is therefore key to gauging the effectiveness of suppliers.

In larger organisations a buyer will probably be supported by an assistant or trainee buyer who will normally be a person who wishes to pursue a career in the field. They will be largely responsible for the organisation of the ranges, perform some clerical work whilst preparing products for garment reviews, monitoring the product development critical path and production milestones, liaising with suppliers and technology as well as deputising for the buyer when they are out of the office.

A point to note is that the relationship between buyers and suppliers often develops into more than a pure business association due to the fact that they spend much time travelling together and working closely with one another building ranges. Close familiar relationships frequently make it difficult to maintain a business like association for the mutual benefit of both parties and can cloud business decision making and judgment. The temptation of bribery and incentives in exchange for placing large orders may be desirous. For newer naïve buyers the rule that the supplier is not your friend should be firmly applied simply because they are more easily seduced by grandiose lunches and gifts as many have unfortunately found out the hard way when they move on and are no longer of great importance to the particular supplier.

A way of balancing the workloads or ranking of buyers and merchandisers is to evaluate the actual number of suppliers, stock keeping units or barcodes being handled by each buyer and then make comparisons regarding workload and productivity of each buyer to established benchmarks.

Merchandisers

The merchandiser or planner applies their focus on maximising profitability from the business end. This is done largely through the analysis of historical sales and the influence of the trend direction to determine the range categories and product breakdown within the overall sales budget.

The role defines what stock levels are required to meet the preset targets such as seasonal stock turnover or forward stock covers based on the sales trends over time. Knowing these requirements, the merchandiser will determine what intake or purchase quantities are needed at any point in time in the season for the total department and each product category.

The level of the budgets will determine the quantity of options in relation to styling, colour palette, size spans, pricing structure and levels of quality per category that will best service the customer for the time that the goods are expected be on offer prior to a new variety of product being introduced in line with the strategic predetermined seasonal themes.

The merchandiser's job has to be to provide guidance to the buyer to procure within the budget parameters. In short it can be described as providing the buyer with a shopping list or range plan that allows them to go out and fill in the blanks on the plan while buying product. This activity requires the careful management of the "open to buy" which can often be a source of tension between the buyer who always tends to want more and the merchandiser who holds the purse strings. A good deal of emotional maturity and teamwork on both sides is therefore critical for a successful partnership.

Sadly the merchandising role is often branded as a dull, boring number crunching task in accordance with mathematical calculations and while it is this, it can be better described as a creative manipulation of numbers. This task is highly rewarding when positive trade results are achieved or alternatively equally as depressing when these do not materialise. The role can be likened to that of a husband who places his entire salary on a dead cert horse at the races which was by no means appreciated by his wife. However when the horse won he was similarly unpopular for not putting more money on the horse!

Like the buying role, the merchandiser deals with different activities simultaneously as part of the team across a number of seasons and therefore requires high levels of multi-tasking and re-prioritising in the forward planning, problem resolution, critical milestone management, analysis and timeous action implementation.

As the actual trade takes place the results need to be carefully analysed and immediate action plans initiated in order to maximise the opportunities and minimise the levels of markdowns that erode the profits. For these reasons they need to be logical, reliable, and consistent in order to take decisions based on fact.

The regular timeous generation of reports detailing sales analysis, stock levels and forward planning needs are distributed to all team members and to senior management. Often numeric information and commercial analysis is demanded on an immediate ad-hoc basis which adds pressure to the job function and can be very disruptive to routines which in such situations requires the merchandiser to adapt quickly and effectively.

The merchandiser plays an integral role during the presentation at product reviews from the numbers perspective which influences the agreed product mix and justification of the levels of sales budgets.

A detailed understanding is necessary of the stores and the customer profile inherent to respective stores that are best met through the attributes of the ranges in terms of styling, colour and size that are put on offer within the store space constraints. The task is best described by the saying "plan each store as if it is your own" which could never be truer.

With sophisticated IT development and the availability of various software packages, some of which may be developed exclusively for the retailer, will provide quick sales analysis, production planning and afford the ability to make sound decisions based on accurate data. This information is especially necessary to give guidance to the allocator or distributor who will be sending the appropriate quantities to satisfy the store's needs as well as give direction as to the level of repeat buys for products that are trading above expectations.

Some organisational structures do differentiate the allocation function between the merchandiser who focuses on the forecasting and production planning and that of the allocator or location planner who will be responsible to distribute the product to the stores in the most appropriate combinations of styles, colour and sizes that meet the store profiles. This function can be housed as an extension within the buying division or may be part of a separate centralised group where an allocator may be responsible for a diverse number of departments. The benefits of such a centralised structure is that there could be a cost saving advantage especially where smaller departments do not warrant a dedicated staff member but added to this is a pool of knowledge which develops a highly skilled team who are able to cross pollinate information, coordinate inter departmental promotions effectively and develop consistent techniques and skills. The identification of common emerging trends will contribute to the optimisation of sales and assist in the control of stock quantities at a very detailed level and thereby maximise profits. Close connections to the departmental merchandisers is maintained to ensure that their actions are aligned to the departmental strategy and plans.

The need for the diversification of the function also makes more sense from the point of view in that where the distribution function is retained within the department it inevitably adds to the increasing workload of the merchandiser. The departmental merchandiser task has more and more been impacted on by the development, the implementation and mastering of complex and sophisticated information systems that analyse sales and stock with added forward planning functionalities.

Many such systems are able to integrate with other supporting IT platforms such as supplier performance, technological measurement, critical path management, ordering, logistical and store systems. The added management of a complex allocation system that is necessary to move the stock to stores is more and more difficult with the result that the incumbent is in danger of being drawn into concentrating on and coping with the intricate detail. As a result, the merchandiser runs the risk of losing sight of the bigger objectives as set out in the strategy and operational plans and the consequent degrading of the inherent merchant intuition becomes very real.

The merchandiser needs to effectively manage and develop the merchandising team which can, not unlike the buying role, consist of an assistant merchandiser or trainee who aspire to be a merchandiser.

The role ensures cohesion of activities that have to be synchronized based on actual sales performance through the formalised interaction with other stakeholders such as the buyers and technologists. This contact is usually in the form of regular, typically weekly, departmental meetings where corrective decisions and plans of action are agreed. Frequent association with the points of sale in stores through written communications and reports as well as formal site visits are critical to keep aligned with the customer's preferences and emerging trends and confirm that the stores are sharing the same vision of the overall strategy.

The need to guide suppliers assertively in terms of prioritisation and the achievement of deadlines is critical to meet the suitable stock requirements at any point in time, particularly in relation to peak seasonal periods or key events. For example, once winter breaks, which it does every year except the exact date is not easy to predict, the objective is to have the right stocks in place such as knitwear, thermal underwear, scarves and the like in sufficient quantities to meet the rush. The usual manner to assist in the anticipation of the weather trend is done through reference to previous years data when the weather changes happened which also help to understand variations in out of ordinary performance at particular times. The challenge is therefore to have the appropriate quantities in the stores at the vital time while the maintenance of the balance of stocks must be adequate to cater for the demand without overstocking the stores ahead of planned stock targets. Events such as Easter, Christmas, Valentine's Day and Mother's day are easier to predict and the right levels of stock can be made more accurately available at the right time.

Where suppliers do not meet the required delivery dates, the merchandiser needs to manage the consequences that have to be applied for the underperformance. This can result in some very sensitive and emotional discussions and the negotiation of penalties typically in the form of discounts, sale or return agreements or even total cancellation which will no doubt impact negatively on both parties.

Technology

Technical Teams consist broadly of the fabric and garment technologists. Fabric technologists are highly trained specialists who focus on typically woven or knitted disciplines. Specialised products such as knitwear, tailoring and footwear require added knowledge of components and specific production machinery.

A major portion of the fabric technologist's task is the development and innovation of new fabrics and the enhancement of existing products. New fibres and blends of fibres such as the blending of natural and synthetic fibres, addition of chemicals to finishing process will possibly lead to new inventions and improvements such as better washability, softer handles, easy care properties like easy to iron, crease resistant finishes, rot resistant applications, seamless or seams that are glued that allow for smoother looks particularly for under garments, the evolvement of elastane products such as lycra which revolutionised active and casual wear and the enhancement of thermal properties of winter undergarments. The success of such developments which add to the profitability as well as the form and function necessitates a close working relationship with suppliers, mills and value adders.

Garment technology have the responsibility to ensure that the make-up of the garment meets the set down criteria and the componentry like buttons, interlinings and threads are of the standard that is functional and are not inferior.

Many factories have developed specified technological capabilities that have been built around the production of a particular category of garments relevant to them which vary from factory to factory or even within the same plant. The garment technologist must understand this implicitly and exploit this knowledge to its fullest.

The relationship with the commercial team is sometimes strained as the ideal level of form and function can be challenged by the need to market the product at the most commercially competitive price.

The objective of the garment technologist is to ensure that quality is not compromised. The tasks essential to achieve this can be varied, for example, the assessment of potential manufacturers and fabric mills to ensure that the established standards are achievable, the specification of raw materials, overseeing sampling stages and ensuring that any delays which may result through the process do not compromise the delivery prerequisites.

In safeguarding that the all quality standards are met particularly through the inspection of garments, inspectors need to possess specific skills. Quality controllers should be ethical, sincere and honest, open mindedly being willing to consider alternatives, be diplomatic and tactful in their dealings with people and are able to actively observe their surroundings as well as perceive and adapt to varying situations.

The technologist has an intimate knowledge of the supplier base through historical awareness as well as from continually researching new and existing suppliers. As the sourcing specialist they have to guide buying teams in the selection of the most appropriate manufacturer for the various types of product. It is also very essential that they are conscious of the fabric prominence for the forthcoming season as dictated by the strategies and budget levels to ensure that there is sufficient capacities at the relevant mills to meet the overall demands without compromising quality.

The task of assessing potentially new suppliers is a role that may be included in the stable of the technical team or it may be hived off to defined sourcing specialists who are knowledgeable team members that recognise the strengths and weaknesses of suppliers and based on this where best to place orders accordingly.

Suppliers are assessed on various criteria such as their management infrastructure, financial stability, specialised equipment availability, fabric specialty, levels of innovation, fashion or basic production orientation, the other retailers they serve, their flexibility of cost negotiability and social responsibility policies. Other external factors that may well influence the selection of suppliers could be those like prevailing exchange rates, remuneration policies and physical locality.

In summary, the significance must be emphasised that the diverse buying teams all have to have a clear informed understanding of each other's roles and priorities and that they are aligned to ensure all their tasks are integrated to achieve the goal of delivering consistent quality products manufactured by appropriately skilled suppliers on time all the time. This is especially imperative in the case of more complex products such as corsetry, tailored garments and knitwear.

The handling, packaging, storage and movement of the product through the supply channels has to be done in such a way that the quality of the product is not allowed to deteriorate in any way whatsoever. As some product is sourced from more distant locations a newer trend is to contract the technical function out to approved independent technical service providers or to trusted garment and fabric suppliers themselves who understand and are committed to the standards required. These service providers are thereby able to approve samples, perform quality control and be responsible for the eventual release of the finished product.

PROCESS FLOW OF KEY RETAIL ACTIVITIES

While a lot of activities are required from conceptualisation to the eventual offering of a completed product to the customer they do nevertheless follow a relative set sequence of events even though there may be at any point in time where they can possibly overlap each other.

In the sections that follow, the detail required for each key activity will be explored and their relationships and dependencies on each other will be highlighted.

The journey commences broadly with strategy formulation and the strategic planning for each stakeholder area, the creation of a merchandise plan through to the buying of the product within the budgetary parameters. The commercial team have the support of the technology teams to establish the technical requirements as well as the sourcing of appropriate suppliers in order to enable the production of the product.

The packaging is detailed to assist in the marketing of the product and protect the garments in transit and storage. Orders are initiated and the critical production milestones are managed in such a way to ensure delivery deadlines are met timeously.

During production the quality inspection and supplier performance management takes place and once the order is complete the products will be allocated and delivered either directly to stores or to a storage facility. In some instances there may be value added processes applied to the goods after which they will be transported to stores.

Once the goods are on offer to the customer the sales are analysed and reviewed in order to make adjustments where necessary. At the end of the season the lessons learnt are noted and applied to the strategy development for the new season.

When there is a clear understanding of what operational activities are required, the plan of action can be outlined to deliver the strategic objectives and thereby satisfy the goals of the strategy in the most effective way.

What is key in formulating the planning strategy is to set down the clear guidelines in the development of the product mix which will be carefully tailored in the right proportions in order to best serve the customer at the various locations and in terms of styling, colour quantities across the sizes at the most acceptable prices.

For this to be done successfully the overall process of planning follows a set of prescribed activities that make up the mechanics of running the business as well as accommodating the other stakeholder strategies. The steps are a flow of taking in the lessons learnt during the previous season and utilising the learnings as input in the formulation of the strategic goals for the future season.

The goals will give guidance in the preparation of the level of budgets determining the product mix and setting up the range plan from which the orders will be placed. Once production has taken place according to the plan the goods will be allocated to the stores taking into account their specific customer characteristics. Sales will be analysed as they occur and as the performance dictates the forward plans will be reviewed and adjusted appropriately.

Diagrammatically the high level key planning steps can be outlined as follows

BUYING GROUP ORGANISATION

A characteristic merchandise hierarchical organisational structure of a retailer is illustrated below where mainstream buying and merchandising function cascades down from the highest platform to the lower department level details. Service areas as depicted on the right hand side of the diagram support the core functions.

Typical buying group organisation chart

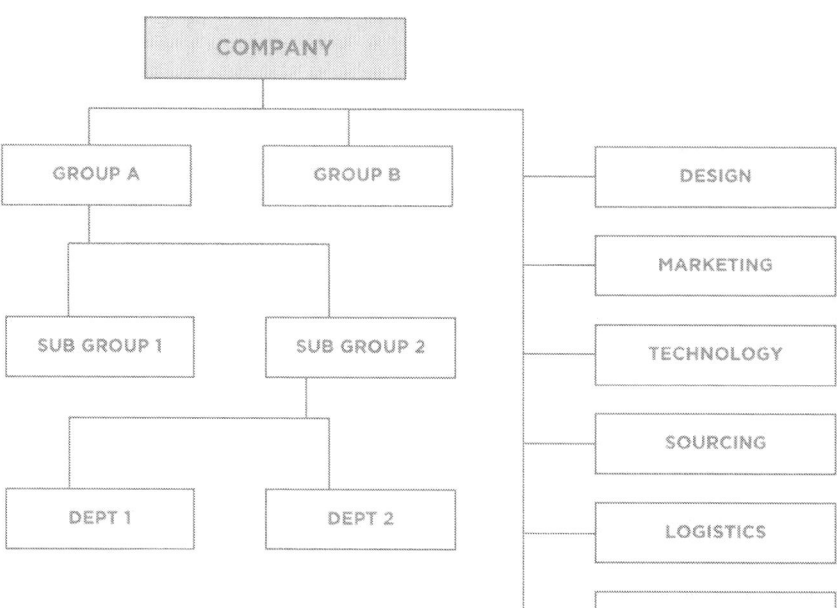

The basic hierarchical staffing roles of all the key players in a mainstream buying structure is outlined diagrammatically below.

The chief executive officer is clearly the leader together with the board of directors who ensure that the overall company strategic intent is delivered and the profits are achieved as reward to the shareholders to whom they are accountable.

Group executives look after the broad category types such as menswear, ladieswear and childrenswear. The responsibility is to ensure that the group delivers to the set strategy and is reacting properly to changing trading conditions while still meeting the profit objective.

Within the mainstream groups such as menswear a sub division into sub groups may well take place probably by lifestyle such as formal wear and casual wear. The category manager is responsible for the mini business or sub group with set turnover targets, profit objectives and strategies.

Buyers, merchandisers and location planners operate at the departmental level down to the lowest degree of product being colour and size and are responsible that the management of the detail delivers the eventual goals at all the higher levels.

Key staffing hierarchy posts of a buying organisation

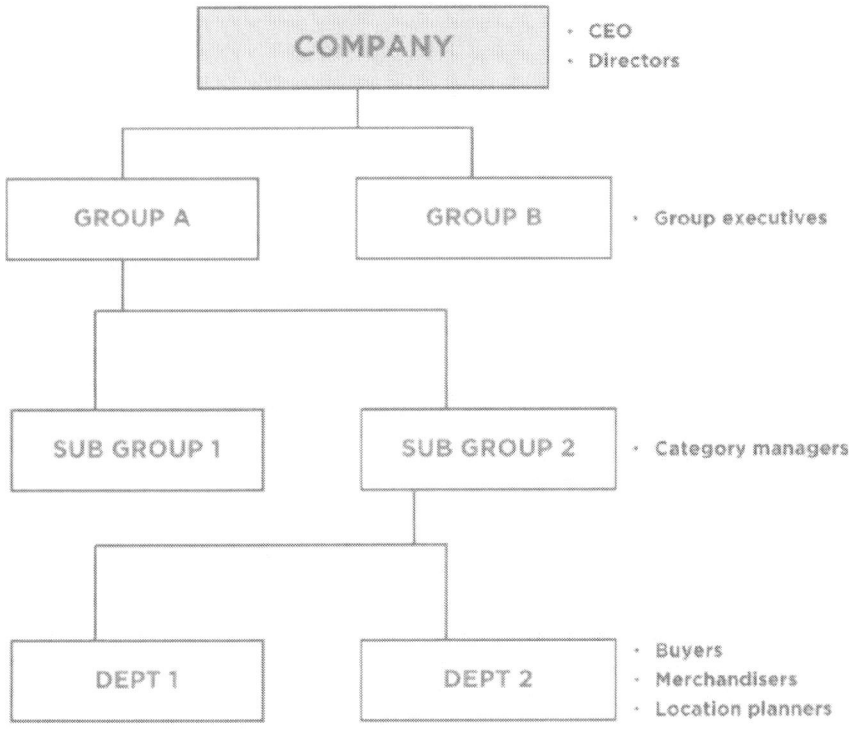

MERCHANDISE PLANNING

There is often confusion as to what merchandise planning actually is and varying interpretations are often touted via a multitude of channels.

A broad brush definition is that it is a systematic approach aimed at maximising return on investment, through planning sales and inventory in order to increase profitability. This is done by the maximisation of sales and the minimisation of markdowns and stock outs.

Merchandise financial planning commences by taking a high level approach in the setting of the sales, margin and inventory targets. Once the high level targets are in place the planning teams then are able to cascade down to the lower hierarchical levels of the product at group, category and line level while integrating it at location level across time.

The principle applied is a top down bottom up approach as will be elaborated upon later. Product planning through the hierarchies is mirrored across locations and time which is sometimes referred to as the retail cube.

Illustratively this can be depicted as follows

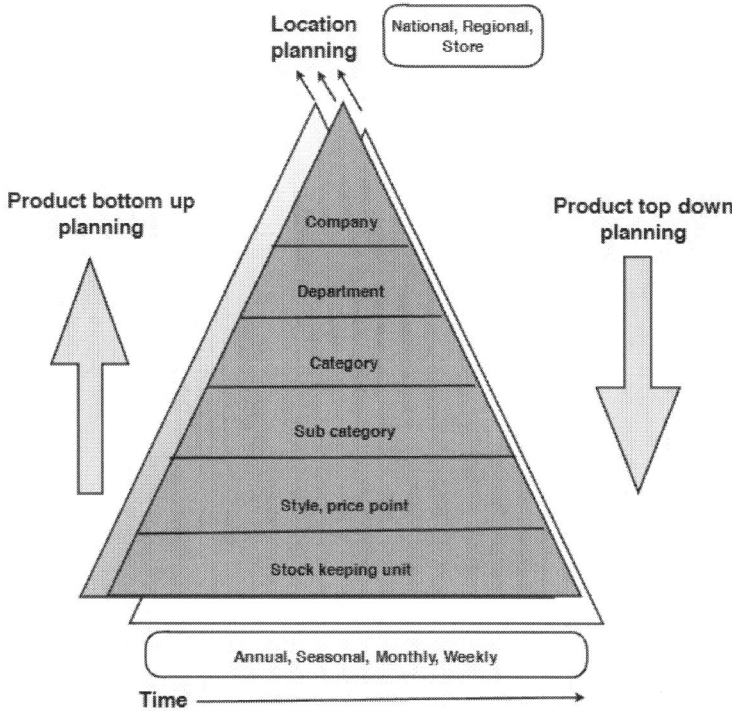

In conjunction with the buyers, designers, sourcing specialists and technologists, the merchandise planner is responsible for the delivery of the departmental strategy to make sure it is aligned to the strategic intent of the company and the group.

The sales forecasting and the planning of the stock levels is done to achieve the sales and margin objectives from departmental level down to the individual product level. Together with the buyer the range planning and building will take place to construct a complete balanced offer of product that satisfies the needs of the target customers.

The intake and orders are carefully controlled to meet the stock requirements as per the plan at any given time while the allocation and distribution of stock is managed in such a way in order to optimise the fulfilment of the customer demands within the selling space available.

The foundation of planning is the manipulation of the components of what is known as the retail balance set which are key to driving out profit.

The balance set components comprise of

- Sales
- Markdowns
- Intake
- Stock

The inter relationship between the balance set components of them can be shown as follows

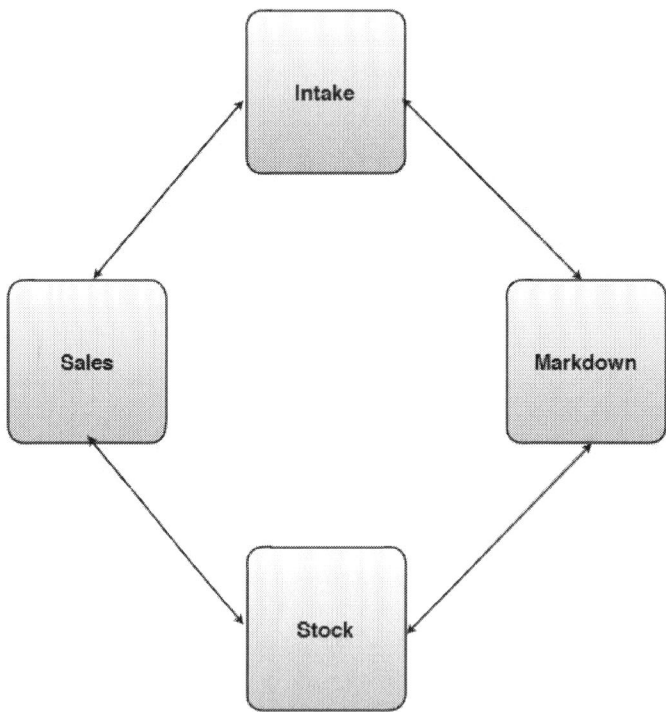

The fundamental calculation rules of the relative components

The common deduction is the necessity to determine how much stock must be bought to meet the planned sales and stock targets or alternatively to consider what the resultant stock levels would be if a pre-determined amount was procured. However the second option is less utilised as invariably the result will be different to that of the original plan.

Assume the components values for a period are

Sales = 1000

Markdowns = 40

Intake = 1240

Closing Stock = 2000

Opening Stock = 1800

Intake = Closing stock plus sales and markdown less opening stock

(2000+1000+40)-1800 = 1240

Closing Stock = Opening Stock less Sales and Markdowns plus Intake

(1800-1000-40)+1240 = 2000

Basic steps of planning process

The principles of planning outlined below is affectionately referred to by some retailers as WISSI which stands for the weekly sales, stock and intake plan. This process has been adopted in some format or other by many merchants worldwide and forms the basis of the logic in technical planning packages which are marketed by a number of software developers. The basic principles are also key to the integration of the planning function with suites of other operational packages such as allocation systems, buying range planning, critical path management, warehousing and distribution applications.

The sequence of steps to determine an intake plan is portrayed as follows

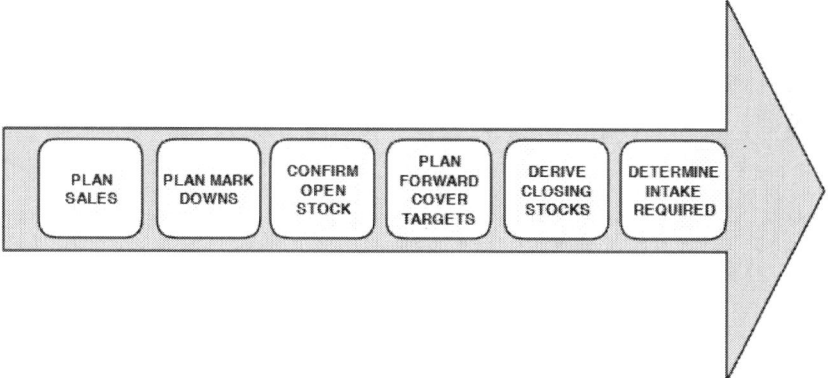

Plan sales

involves the forecasting of sales across time, usually for a six monthly season by month by week in a shape that resembles past history and accounts for any strategic intent such as new product launches, store openings, competitive activity and special events like significant world sports happenings and environmental initiatives. It needs to be recognised that some occasions take place at different times from year to year such as Easter and Eid and should be provided for accordingly.

Statistical methods of sales forecasting commonly use the exponential smoothing of trends or weighted moving average options in simple models which are relatively easy to use. For more complex scenarios such as with the introduction of new categories or catering for products with erratic sales it is likely that the predictions will include a safety stock factor to cater for the unexpected. In such cases some companies utilise experts or rely on advanced software to assist in the analysis and formulation of expected patterns.

It should be noted that the combination of the individual product life cycles are overlaid across time to accumulate the formation of the upper level sales pattern.

The traditional life cycle of a product may be illustrated as follows

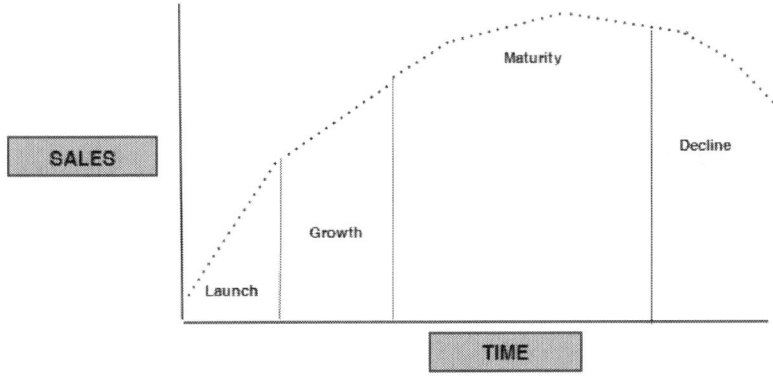

Plan markdowns

is required as it is inevitable that not all goods will sell as expected which means that the clearance of oddments is necessary in order to facilitate the flow of newness and other promotional activities as well as relieve any space constraints.

The level of provision for markdowns that is set is influenced by historical trends and the characteristics of the product. The higher the fashionability of the category, the greater is the risk and therefore for such products a higher markdown allowance is necessary. The converse applies for basic continuity product. While it is usually quite easy to accurately predict the amount of acceptable markdown at the higher departmental level, the markdown value contribution of individual line products can differ considerably to expectations.

Traditional types of markdown are the typical end of season cleanouts where there is an aggressive campaign to remove the unwanted product to provide for the introduction of a new seasons launch or for a promotional product sale as part of a strategic intent.

The argument exists that although the regular sell off of products attracts more feet in the store and stimulates the sale of regular priced goods while freeing up space for new launches the customer soon understands the strategy and adapts buying patterns.in order to benefit from the inevitable reduction.

The sell through plan of the sale depends on the intended time the affected goods are placed on offer with scheduled phases of further intermittent reductions and a final liquidation at the end of the period. The general trend that exists as a rule of thumb is that most of the fashion and brand retailers sell fifty to sixty percent of their stock at full price while the rest of the merchandise is sold at discounts of thirty to fifty percent eroding approximately twenty percent of margin while the balance is virtually written off.

Illustratively the markdown activity with probable examples of periods and percentage cuts can be represented as follows.

The progressive phases of markdown sales

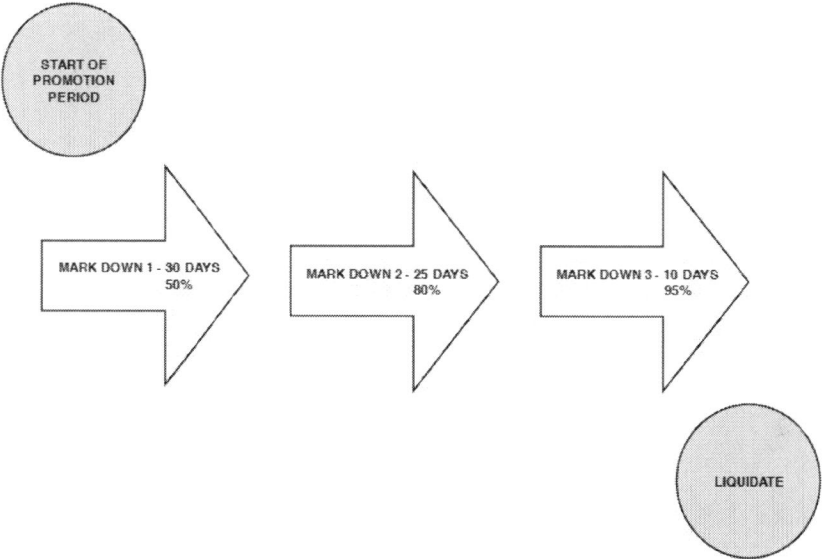

Planned promotions

should always have a structured post mortem assessment. The framework of the analysis could possibly be done by measuring by how much sales improve for a set period after the promotional launch compared to the level of sales prior to the campaign.

A selection of similar products can be earmarked as control items to which an evaluation can be made in terms of the uplift in sales experienced versus the sales of the control items as well as what the effect of possible substitution purchases were during the same period. Based on these findings the conclusion may be drawn as to the success and viability in terms of increase in profit and market penetration.

Consideration should be given to the space constraints in tight metreage stores to accommodate aggressive promotions. If the volumes and number of customer choices are too great, it may result in the operational efficiencies of the store being compromised and will result in the layout becoming disconnected from the strategic intent. In these instances it may be considered to transfer some or all of the reduced stock to larger stores.

Confirm opening stock

The starting point for stock represents the actual value of closing stock in the previous period. This has to be recognised as the value affects the required intake particularly in the early part of the new season and may well also have an impact on the level of planned markdown that subsequently may need to be reviewed.

In the illustration below the planned opening stock for week 1 is 7000 more than the actual open stock of 70000 and therefore the intake will have to increase by 7000 to keep in line with the planned closing stock of 79000

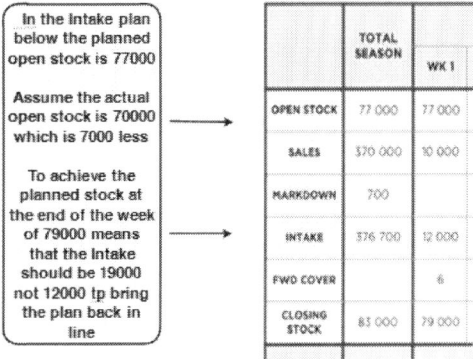

Plan forward cover targets

based on the acceptable number of weeks that are strategically agreed for the various categories of products which will aid the achievement of the approved stock turn.

	TOTAL SEASON	MONTH 1				MO	
		WK 1	WK 2	WK 3	WK 4	WK 5	WK 6
OPEN STOCK	77 000	77 000	79 000	82 000	81 000	81 000	88 000
SALES	370 000	10 000	12 000	14 000	14 000	12 000	13 000
FWD COVER		6	6	6	6	6	6

> In wk 1 the planned open stock is 77000
>
> The fwd wks cover is set at 6
>
> Adding up the sales for the fwd 6 weeks gives a required opening stock of 77000 in wk 1

Derive closing stock values

using the number of weeks forward cover at the end of each month and apply them to the weekly sales plan going forward.

Determine the intake required

through the balanced set calculation of closing stock plus sales and markdown less opening stock for each month and the total season.

It should be noted that the weekly sales into the early part of the next season should be taken into account in order to calculate the closing stock targets to meet the forward cover requirements.

In the construction of the simplified model of the intake plan below a flat forward cover of six weeks has been selected for ease of illustration. In reality it may change in the event of special happenings such as factory closures over holiday periods when the routine distribution is disrupted or there is stock build up requirement for new initiative launches, packaging change overs, catalogue adjustments and new store openings.

A representative example of the intake plan

	TOTAL SEASON	MONTH 1				MONTH 2				MONTH 3				
		WK 1	WK 2	WK 3	WK 4	WK 5	WK 6	WK 7	WK 8	WK 9	WK 10	WK 11	WK 12	WK 13
OPEN STOCK	77 000	77 000	79 000	82 000	81 000	81 000	88 000	96 000	98 000	98 000	99 000	98 000	91 000	83 000
SALES	370 000	10 000	12 000	14 000	14 000	12 000	13 000	14 000	15 000	13 000	14 000	19 000	21 000	16 000
MARKDOWN	700				700									
INTAKE	376 700	12 000	15 000	13 000	14 700	19 000	21 000	16 000	15 000	14 000	13 000	12 000	13 000	15 000
FWD COVER		6	6	6	6	6	6	6	6	6	6	6	6	6
CLOSING STOCK	83 000	79 000	82 000	81 000	81 000	88 000	96 000	98 000	98 000	99 000	98 000	91 000	83 000	82 000

	TOTAL SEASON	MONTH 4				MONTH 5				MONTH 6			
		WK 14	WK 15	WK 16	WK 17	WK 18	WK 19	WK 20	WK 21	WK 22	WK 23	WK 24	WK 25	WK 26
OPEN STOCK	77 000	82 000	83 000	84 000	85 000	86 000	87 000	87 000	85 000	83 000	83 000	85 000	85 000	83 000
SALES	370 000	15 000	14 000	13 000	12 000	13 000	15 000	16 000	15 000	14 000	13 000	14 000	15 000	14 000
MARKDOWN	700													
INTAKE	376 700	16 000	15 000	14 000	13 000	14 000	15 000	14 000	13 000	14 000	15 000	14 000	13 000	14 000
FWD COVER		6	6	6	6	6	6	6	6	6	6	6	6	6
CLOSING STOCK	83 000	83 000	84 000	85 000	86 000	87 000	87 000	85 000	83 000	83 000	85 000	85 000	83 000	83 000

Monthly financial planning

As part of the preparation of the intake plan it is good practice to present a basic month by month financial plan for the department. This will enable all the department month by month plans to be rolled up to group level and then all groups can be consolidated to total company level. A clear picture of the financial requirements to run the business is thereby provided to senior management and enables the arrangements for the liquidity of funds necessary for each month.

The merchandise financial plan facilitates the high level plan for the total organisation through the accumulation of all the lower level plans. Through this the organisations traditional open to buy requirement across the planning calendar across time can be determined.

Using the values from the intake plan above the financial planning summary will look as follows

DEPARTMENTAL MONTHLY FINANCIAL SUMMARY

	OPEN STOCK	SALES	MARKDOWN	INTAKE	CLOSE STOCK
MONTH 1	77 000	50 000	700	54 700	81 000
MONTH 2	81 000	54 000		71 000	98 000
MONTH 3	98 000	83 000		67 000	82 000
MONTH 4	82 000	54 000		46 200	85 000
MONTH 5	85 000	59 000		70 000	83 000
MONTH 6	83 000	56 000		56 000	83 000

The determination of intake required is applicable at any product hierarchy level. The highest platform would be for the total company which then flows down to group and department. Thereafter it can be drilled down to product level and subsequently to colour and size.

The same holds true for location planning from total company through to regional and store level.

The principle of top down planning and bottom up verification is key to accurate forecasting. Experience shows that should planning be done from bottom up with a consolidation to a higher level, it is inevitable that the original overall top level plan will be exceeded. If each line is considered in isolation, the reality of the influencing factors such as late deliveries, unforeseen obstacles and events are discounted and will therefore invariably deliver a much more optimistic plan. The added danger of a bottom up approach could possibly result in uncertainty or mistrust of the strategy and therefore plans with excessive percentage increases on last year should be challenged and be given careful consideration and validation.

A point to remember is that budgets cannot be banked and it seems to be a natural tendency of human nature to be optimistic and endeavour to justify higher budget levels. It is important to remain as realistic as possible in the setting of the financial plan levels.

The challenge of chasing products where performance is above expectation is far more pleasurable than frantically switching off production and suffering the consequences of over commitments which may be in the form of completed product or raw materials. The threat of suppliers having to work shorter hours or needing to retrench production staff can also become a real possibility.

Plans should be realistic in terms of the transition from a preceding season into a new season. Formulating budgets in isolation comes with the dogged assumption that the errors of the previous season will not be repeated nor will there be any misjudgments going forward. The expectation is also that the benefits which will be enjoyed through new initiatives and products are over and above current levels of performance. The reality is however that this does not happen from day one when at midnight of the last day of the previous season the mediocre level of sales will instantly transform into a higher optimistic level of performance almost as if a message was shot off to all customers to tell them to start buying more.

Another common trap is that during the formulation of the strategy and operational plan the desires are considered to be a given and it is assumed without doubt that it is going to happen. A common example is the want to generate higher levels of profit which may be done through the adjustment of the margin policy upwards and inevitably selling prices as well. It is presumed that the change will be happily accepted by customers and intake plans are then put in place to meet the revised targets. The unfortunate inevitability is that the changeover does not happen immediately from day one of the new season as it takes a time for customers to digest and possibly modify buying habits. Consequently disillusionment amongst the retail team reigns which results in strategy and sales plans being questioned and a resultant panic plan to rectify the situation is implemented at an early stage.

During the trading period the actual values will differ to the planned expectations and the anticipated values need to be substituted with the actual. The plan going forward consequently needs to be adjusted based on a different opening stock, changed markdown value and therefore requires that the intake value to be adjusted in order to bring the plan back in line.

Where performance is not up to standard, the product mix of the intake going forward may still remain well-matched to the plan in terms of any new coordinated ranges and seasonal launches. In order to ensure that this is done effectively it could be necessary to consider other options whereby stock levels may be allowed to drift above planned levels for a time and to be gradually brought back in line to realistic targets.

A worthy practice is to permit for spare open to buy right up to the latest point in time before committing in contract form. Such a tactic will facilitate the pursuit of the better selling lines or being able to absorb growing overstocks thus maintaining tighter stock controls and avoiding possible financial disaster.

Integration of hierarchy level plans

Product plans from a company level down to individual product group by week need to be integrated with the location planning hierarchy in order that the stores are stocked with the most appropriate assortment of product to effectively satisfy the customer needs.

The same principle applies in location plans that the higher hierarchical levels are considered to be the most accurate to lay down the parameters to which plans from the lower levels are balanced back to.

The integration of plans is illustrated below

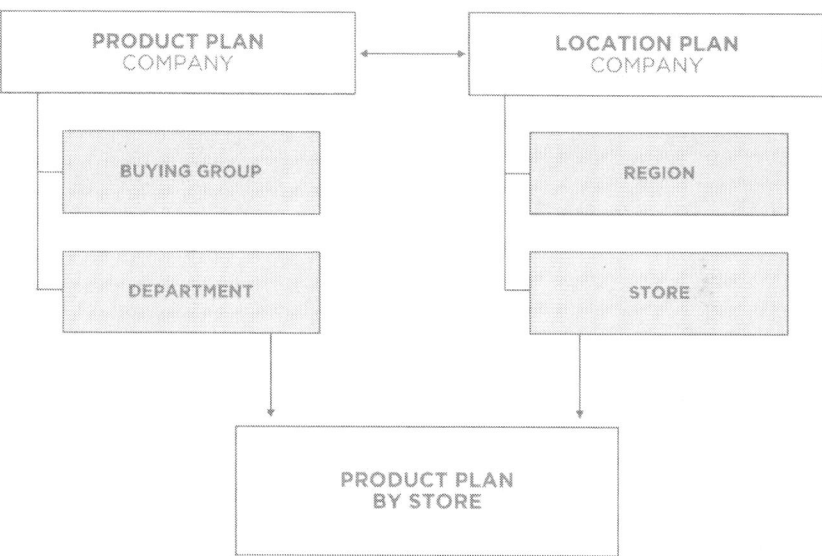

Location plans

In setting up the location plans it is important to be aware of what products are going to which stores and be sure that they are in suitable proportions and quantities that will best service the unique customer profiles that are applicable to the individual stores. The store profile or personality will be influenced predominantly by the surrounding economic factors, lifestyles and cultural demographics. A common technique to consider is to cluster similar profile stores into specific groupings so that they all carry like catalogues of products which will assist in the efficiency of planning and achieve a comparable handwriting across the chain.

A logical way to define the accurate range of product types as well as give guidance to the quantities for the right places is through the drafting of a matrix which indicates the correct kind of products that are to be destined to different groups of stores. In principle there is a base selection of product that would go to all stores and thereafter selected products which will be earmarked for specific store profile groups dependent on factors such as sales budgets, space constraints, layout plans, price sensitivity and fashion demands. The main purpose is to ensure that a store receives the correct width of range based on the store's unique characteristics and future expected performance.

A simple example of such a matrix could look as follows

DEPARTMENT XYZ	STORE PROFILE Group A	STORE PROFILE Group B	STORE PROFILE Group C	STORE PROFILE Group D	STORE PROFILE Group E
PRODUCT 1	X	X	X	X	X
PRODUCT 2	X	X	X	X	X
PRODUCT 3	X	X	X	X	X
PRODUCT 4	X	X	X	X	X
PRODUCT 5	X	X	X	X	X
PRODUCT 6	X	X	X		
PRODUCT 7	X	X	X	X	
PRODUCT 8	X	X			
PRODUCT 9	X	X			X
PRODUCT 10	X				

Realistic sales plans by subclass for each store are put in place which eventually rolls up to the location plan at a total department level which provides a guideline for the number of choices that should be planned for each store grouping.

New stores or stores with partial sales history are also planned in the location plans taking into account like profile stores, like turnovers, the store opening date and the overall location planned sales and the stores average unit sales by style.

The location plan delivers the store sales plans by subclass over time, the store groupings by subclass down to style level over time.

Once the store plans are completed and are rolled up to the total location plan the requirement is that they need to be reconciled to the department merchandise plan at corporate subclass level which enables the department strategic intent to be taken into account and provide a sales shape across time to ensure store and product growths are planned similarly.

An underlying standard which needs to be understood is that planning is a constantly changing iterative process that requires continual pre-season and in-season review dependent on customers, competitors and suppliers behaving differently to what was anticipated. Other factors may be renovations, store format changes, modernisations, revamps etc. that have to be taken into account in the location plan.

The eighty twenty rule

A point of consideration that should never be ignored is the eighty twenty rule, also known as the Pareto principle where it is acknowledged that eighty percent of the result is delivered by twenty percent of the effort or participants.

In the context of stores it is probable that twenty percent of the stores deliver eighty percent of the sales and deserve the proportionate dedication of energy and focus, as does the thick middle sizes such as medium and large and therefore should always be in stock. Core base colours such as white, black, naturals and greys also contribute largely to the sales and should always be evident in volume. It is clear that certain styling features will likewise guarantee the bulk of sales and should be finalised first and certain peak trading periods such as holidays or special events will contribute largely to the total seasonal sales and must be managed very carefully in terms of production planning and delivery scheduling.

It should be qualified that it is not necessarily exactly a ratio of eighty versus twenty as in certain cases it could be a ninety to ten or seventy to thirty relationship but nevertheless the principle still holds true.

Sophisticated merchandise planning applications

Many retailers are still reliant on basic spreadsheets or outdated planning applications to conduct business.

The use of sophisticated, high technical retail planning solutions without doubt bring with it a number of benefits enabling the retailer to have a competitive advantage with a greater level of efficiency.

Some of the major benefits is that there is a far greater degree of accuracy with one version of the truth as data is integrated across a number of systems which eliminates the continual disputes trying to agree which systems data is correct. The converse, however, also exists in that if the data is wrong from the source it is wrong everywhere.

Various consistent views can be created with spreadsheet capabilities that are able to be rolled up or down through and reconciled across all hierarchies which includes historical data. These features accommodate forecasting and hind sighting capabilities as well as facilitate collaboration with other platforms such as logistics.

Data is seamlessly linked across all plans and is particularly beneficial to planning and action of assortment and allocation plans which can facilitate flexible "what if" planning.

A vital requirement is that such systems must be user friendly and easy to use which allows the planner to complete tasks more quickly. The danger exists that if this requirement is not met the mastering of the system becomes the prime objective of the user rather than the focus on true merchanting.

MERCHANDISE ASSORTMENT PLANNING

The assortment of product carried in a retailer's store at any point in time is defined by the types of product on offer. The primary goal of effective assortment planning is to specify a mix of product that will maximise the sales and gross margin.

There are a variety of issues that have to be considered to make a proper determination and the decision making processes subject to several different conditions. These conditions may include issues such as a limited budget for purchase of products, restricted available shelf space for displaying products, seasonal items, holiday selling cycles and a variety of other miscellaneous constraints.

Assortment planning needs to take into account the typical profiles that the retailer is servicing. The seasonal introduction of new products, brands and trends based on continually changing consumer tastes. This frequently necessitates buyers and designers to consult with trend forecasting companies and other sources to assist.

In essence the SKU's or stock keeping units that that exist are segmented into categories such as Menswear and thereafter into sub categories such as Mens casualwear and thereafter into departments, product groups down to products which are defined by style, colour and size which is the fundamental SKU level.

It is critical that the assortment plan reflects the appropriate mix in terms of width and depth of product mix where the continuity and newness of products is a balance by which the consumers are adequately catered for.

The range summary

is required to establish a broad framework. It consists of the initial drafting of a matrix of the mix of product to give guidance of the construction of the range plan which is the range strategy forming part of the department strategy. The source of inputs for the range strategy is the information in the existing range plan, the group strategy and budgets as well as lessons learnt during the previous season.,

A guideline of the number of customer choices in each sub class of product with no volumes attached, the catalogue of stores the customer choices will service over the various time phases will be reflected in the range summary.

The example of a range strategy in the form of a tick sheet is depicted as follows

SKIRTS	Product type	Jan.	Feb.	Mar.	Apr.	May	June
Style 1	Cont	x	x	x	x	x	x
Style 2	Volume	x	x	x			
Style 3	Volume				x	x	x
Style 4	Volume	x	x	x			
Style 5	Volume				x	x	x
Style 6	Input	x					
Style 7	Input		x				
Style 8	Input			x			
Style 9	Input				x		
Style 10	Input					x	
Style 11	Input						x
No of options		4	4	4	4	4	4

> The number of styles in total is 11 but equates to 4 per time period for this specific selection of stores

Once the framework is in place the process of forming the content of the range in terms of the attributes and theme of the range has to be constructed.

The main players in this process are the designers, buyers and technologists.

Design briefs

are made up of significant trend and brand information which are constructed by the design team that include information such as anticipated key silhouettes within the assortments and colour themes, fabric types, print influences and technical direction which will be distributed to buying, planning, technology and sourcing teams.

The brief takes the form of a presentation with the use of story boards and flow charts with description of the themes.

Design concept workshops are set up with relevant stakeholders that may or may not include suppliers with appropriate samples, materials and artwork out of which seasonal concept story boards will evolve by department or brand that will depict the expected themes, key looks for the season, colour pallets, styles and fabric types that will be dominant

A simple example of a typical story board ladies fashion highlighting looks, colour pallette, fabrics and themes is illustrated below

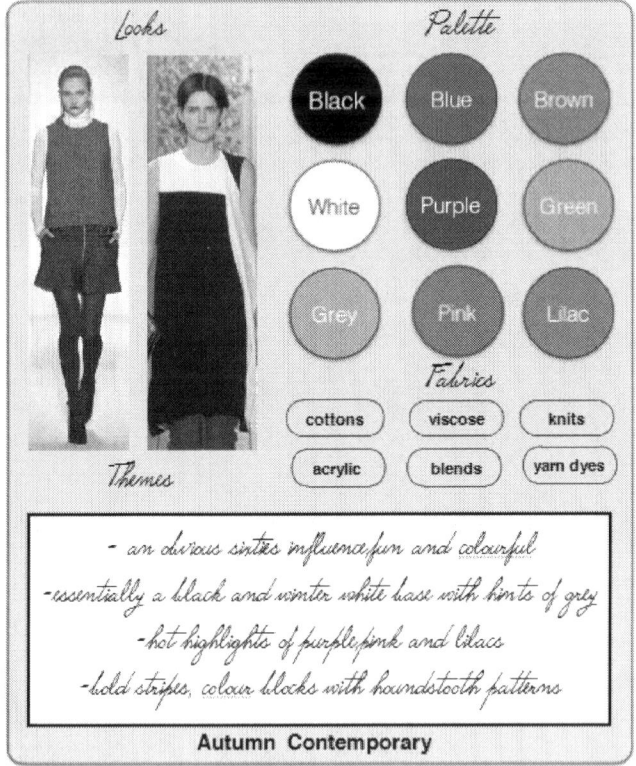

After the design brief is completed and is signed off by the senior management team, buying, design and trend teams commence the conducting of product workshops.

Trend versus fad

There is often confusion in the distinction as to what is a trend and that which is a fad. To distinguish between the two, a trend is a popular general direction which takes longer to build than a fad and lasts longer for which there is a bigger demand. The fad generally has a smaller demand and seldom migrates into the mainstream and characteristically generates a very high rate of interest for a very short period of time and is often just a flash in the pan. To draw a comparison belted waists for dresses may be seen as a trend for an entire season or longer but "oncies" all in one fleece garments for men were a fad that did not last very long.

Trends are driven by attributes such as a specific look, a lifestyle, a colour, fabric, style, a shape or innovation. It is crucial that a trend is accepted by the target customer in that they need to understand an embrace the trend as well as the fact that the style can be adapted for mass appeal.

The trend must be able to be accommodated in the existing price structure and have an acceptable amount of risk that will blend into the overall range.

Product workshops

aim to build a balanced assortment for the season which is aligned to the strategies as set down and meet the range summary.

In these workshops the following will take place

- Samples, artwork and prototypes will be reviewed and approved or rejected
- The colour palettes will be set across the customer segmentations, core continuity products and fashion assortments
- The continuity, core and input items will be confirmed
- Gaps or outstanding items will be identified for which appropriate designs need to sourced

The volumes per customer choice at sub class level is provided by the planning arm and the buyer will decide which product will be assigned to the choice option.

The responsibilities of the main participants in the product workshop is illustrated as follows

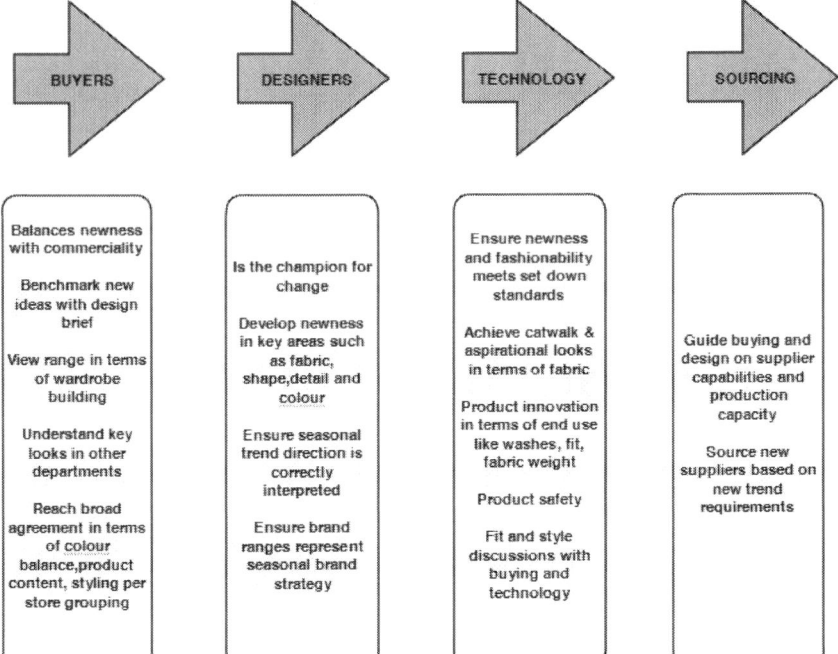

Suppliers

are briefed and will submit appropriate samples according to the design brief pack for consideration in terms of the requirements that have emerged out of the product workshops. If the submissions are successful the samples will be finalised and accepted.

After the products are finalised, the formal contractual procurement process will commence.

Department line sales summary

Prior to the building of the range or buying plan there must be an indication of the expected item sales in money value and units as well as the relative proportion splits across the range for the various store catalogues with the relative variances between this year and last year for the sales value, units and price which will all serve as the preliminary basis for discussion and provide the guidance for the formulation of the intake and range plan.

Price moves highlight whether the inflationary indications are at acceptable levels particularly where products are identical to the previous year and the like for like percentage move is at least in line or is less than the consumer price index.

An example of a line by line summary is as follows

PROD NO	DESCRIPTION	STORE CATALOGUE	SELLING PRICE			SALES '000			SALES UNITS		
			LY	TY	% inc/dec	LY	TY	% inc/dec	LY	TY	% inc/dec
	PROD GROUP 1										
1001	Style ABCD	All	95.00	99.99	5.2%	680 000	730 000	5.7%	7 158	7 300	2.0%
2001	Style ABCE	All	125.00	129.99	4.0%	500 000	550 000	10.0%	4 000	4 231	5.7%
	PROD GROUP 2										
1002	Style ABCF	All	175.00	180.00	2.9%	299 000	350 000	17.0%	1 708	1 944	13.8%
2002	Style ABCG	All	175.00	180.00	2.9%	345 000	400 000	15.9%	1 971	2 222	12.8%
3001	Style ABCH	All	175.00	180.00	2.9%	365 000	390 000	6.8%	2 085	2 027	9.7%
TOTAL DEPARTMENT			129.40	136.53	5.5%	2 189 000	2 420 000	10.6%	16 922	17 724	4.7%

Building the range plan

The construction of a range plan may commence once the financial targets are available through the product and store plans together with a store catalogue matrix. The range plan enables the drafting of a so called "shopping list" for the buying team to be able to fill in the blanks as they make their selections.

The purpose of the range plan is to ensure that the offer of commercial and all-inclusive product ranges meet the needs of all customers. This is done through the combination of the elements of science which covers the planning aspect and art that represents the buying function. To expand further, the scientific practice delivers the clarity of the range offer, the quantities of style and colour levels with the correct pricing policies that support structured cataloguing which meet the varying customer profile pools. The artistic involvement delivers beautiful product and style in categories offering real choice in a way that they are easy to shop. The determination to achieve a successful balanced combination will assist in the potential maximisation of sales and profit as well as undoubtedly help to grow market share.

The philosophies of building a range is the procedure of analysing the historical sales of product categories as well as heeding the lessons learnt from previous seasons and being guided by the strategic definitions. Modifications to the current range structures could be done to compensate for missed opportunities, lost sales through uncommon adversities which should be accounted for as is the need to cater for inflated sales as a result of upcoming out of the norm special events.

Stages of building the range

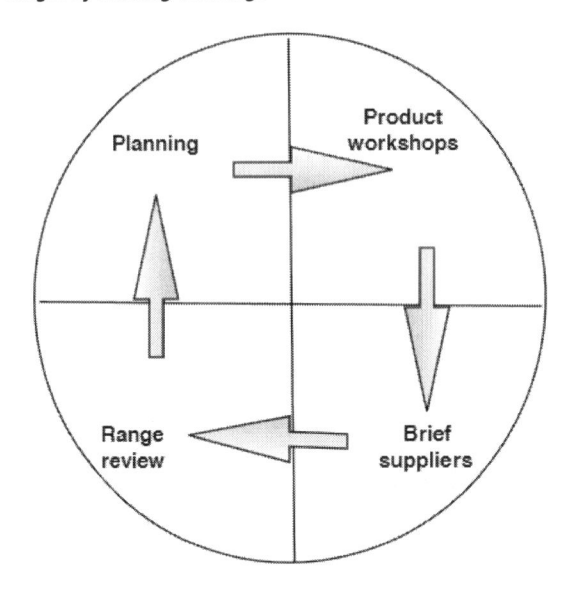

```
        Planning  →  Product workshops
           ↑              ↓
      Range review  ←  Brief suppliers
```

Planning

begins with the range strategy document or matrix tick sheet which covers the customer choices across the period in time such as the season for six months for both the spring/summer and autumn/winter periods.

This stage is completed by the buyer and planner with reference to the group and departmental strategy.

Buyers give consideration to the historical sales, lessons learnt, customer and market shifts to determine the ideal flow of products to accommodate the continuity and input lines utilising the understanding of actual sales, customer needs and marketing plan.

Planners consider the history and lessons learnt, strategy, budgets, volumes, and the frequency of newness and catalogue shifts.

The buyers and planners then agree a final version of the range plan within the parameters of the intake budget.

Product workshops

are conducted to identify the continuity items which represent the building blocks of the department, the highlighting of those products which can be seen as those that will take the department to new levels that prevent the ranges becoming stagnant, incorporating the new fashion trends which potentially could result in new shifts and ensure an appropriate level of balance between newness and traditional continuity items.

Briefing of suppliers

is usually done through the compilation of a briefing pack containing quality information which enables the supplier to clearly understand the thinking of the department and get it right the first time in terms of product development. To do this effectively, the communication has to be clear and details of components, fabrics and styling features have to be simply specified. A good habit to utilise is to reference previous styles or samples.

Range reviews

or final workshops are the conclusion point where the product selected is compared to the original agreed concepts and strategies to decide whether or not any changes need to be made. A cross check needs to be done to make sure that the competitive or sales environment have not altered in any significant way and plans must to be adjusted accordingly. The sequencing of the range and volumes is confirmed to ensure that all end uses are catered for, that products do not compete with each other and the categories are balanced. Lastly the range should be built from bottom up across the various groupings of stores to determine how the product will be represented across the entire chain.

The right product at the right time in the right place in the right quantities and the influences that affect these attributes is illustrated below

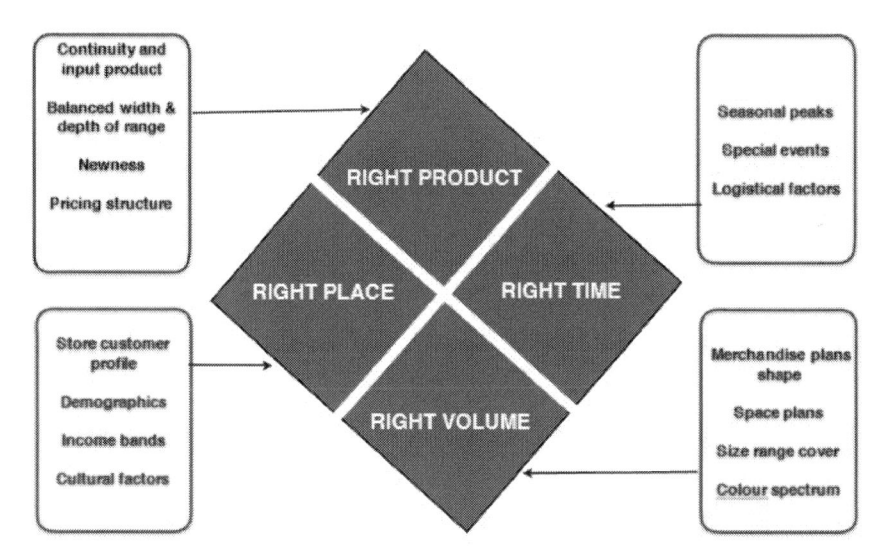

A balance of the right product mix between the basic range types and the fashion inputs has to be determined. The large volume items should be the first focus to ensure that the relevant high money takers are looked after adequately. Second is the necessity to correctly identify the characteristics of fashion forward goods for each product category in order that they best meet the respective store groupings customer profiles and reflect good relative value in comparison to other internal or external products.

The end goal is best summarised by the well-worn quote of having the right product at the right time in the right place in the right quantities.

A simple range plan model based on the guidelines reflected in the departmental line summary above is illustrated on the next page.

Department XYZ Range Plan										Month 1				Month 2				Month 3				
Product Group	Style	Colour	Stores	Cont /Input	Cost price	Sell price	Intake margin	Intake sell value	Intake units	Week 1	Week 2	Week 3	Week 4	Week 5	Week 6	Week 7	Week 8	Week 9	Week 10	Week 11	Week 12	Week 13
1	1001	White	All	Cont	46.99	99.99	53%	250000	2500	150	175	200	225	125	175	200	275	150	200	200	175	250
		Black	All	Cont	46.99	99.99	53%	200000	2000	120	140	160	180	100	140	160	230	120	160	160	140	200
		Blue	Grp A,B,C	Cont	46.99	99.99	53%	160000	1600	96	112	128	144	80	112	128	176	96	128	128	112	160
		Purple	Grp A,B	Cont	46.99	99.99	53%	120000	1200	72	84	96	108	60	84	96	132	72	96	96	84	120
	2001	Beige	All	Cont	63.69	129.99	51%	300000	2308	138	162	165	208	115	162	185	254	136	185	185	162	231
		White	All	Cont	63.69	129.99	51%	250000	1923	115	135	154	173	96	135	154	212	115	154	154	135	192
		Green	Grp A	Cont	63.69	129.99	51%	100000	768	46	46	54	61	38	54	61	84	46	61	61	54	77
Product group 1		Intake units							12300	738	861	981	1107	615	861	981	1353	738	984	984	861	1230
		Intake selling value						1380000		82800	96600	110400	124200	69000	96600	110400	151800	82800	110400	110400	96600	138000
		Merchandise intake plan						1380500		82830	96635	110440	124245	69025	96635	110440	151835	82830	110440	11044	96635	138050
2	1002	Purple	All	Input	82.81	180	54%	150000	833	708		125										
		Yellow	All	Input	82.81	180	54%	120000	667	567		100										
		Orange	Grp A,B	Input	82.81	180	54%	80000	444	378		67										
	2002	Pink	All	Input	82.81	180	54%	170000	944					803		142						
		Brown	All	Input	82.81	180	54%	140000	778					661		117						
		Black	Grp A,B	Input	82.81	180	54%	100000	556					472		83						
	3001	Green	All	Input	82.81	180	54%	190000	1066									897		158		
		White	All	Input	82.81	180	54%	170000	944									803		142		
		Grey	Grp A,B	Input	82.81	180	54%	130000	722									614		108		
Product group 2		Intake units							6944	1853		393		1936		342		2314		408		
		Intake selling value						1250000		297500		52500		348500		61500		416500		73500		
		Merchandise intake plan						1250100		297600		52400		348700		61600		416400		73400		
3	1003	Purpl	All	Input	103.42	220	53%	180000	682	580		102										
		Yellow	All	Input	103.42	220	53%	170000	773	657		116										
		Orange	Grp A,B	Input	103.42	220	53%	120000	546	464		82										
	2003	Pink	All	Input	103.42	220	53%	170000	773					657		116						
		Brown	All	Input	103.42	220	53%	190000	864					734		130						
		Black	Grp A,B	Input	103.42	220	53%	130000	591					502		89						
	3002	Green	All	Input	103.42	220	53%	180000	808									685		123		
		White	All	Input	103.42	220	53%	170000	783									667		116		
		Grey	Grp A,B	Input	103.42	220	53%	130000	591									502		89		
Product group 3		Intake units							6411	1701		300		1893		335		1854		328		
		Intake selling value						1410000		374220		65000		416500		73500		408000		72000		
		Merchandise intake plan						1410100		374010		65920		416800		73450		408020		72100		
Total Dept XYZ		Intake units							23665	4292	861	1573	1107	4444	861	1658	1353	4906	984	1720		
		Intake selling value						4040000		754520	96600	227900	124200	834000	96600	245400	151800	907300	110400	255900		
		Merchandise intake plan						4040700		754440	96635	228760	124245	834525	96635	245490	151835	907250	110440	156544		

For clarification of the range plan section A provides all the key data of the product in terms of product group in terms of the department's product group, style, colour, sore catalogue, whether the style is a fashion input or is a replenishment continuity line, the cost and selling price as well the resultant intake margin. The total intake value and intake units represents the "buy".

The intake value and unit buy is summarised at the product group and total level with a comparison to the merchandise intake plan which delivers the alignment status between the assortment plan and the merchandise financial plan.

Section A

Department XYZ Range Plan

Product Group	Style	Colour	Stores	Cont /input	Cost price	Sell price	Intake margin	Intake sell value	Intake units
1	1001	White	All	Cont	46.99	99.99	53%	250000	2500
		Black	All	Cont	46.99	99.99	53%	200000	2000
		Blue	Grp A,B,C	Cont	46.99	99.99	53%	160000	1600
		Purple	Grp A,B	Cont	46.99	99.99	53%	120000	1200
	2001	Beige	All	Cont	63.69	129.99	51%	300000	2308
		White	All	Cont	63.69	129.99	51%	250000	1923
		Green	Grp A	Cont	63.69	129.99	51%	100000	768
Product group 1			Intake units						12300
			Intake selling value					1380000	
			Merchandise intake plan					1380500	
2	1002	Purple	All	Input	82.81	180	54%	150000	833
		Yellow	All	Input	82.81	180	54%	120000	667
		Orange	Grp A,B	Input	82.81	180	54%	80000	444
	2002	Pink	All	Input	82.81	180	54%	170000	944
		Brown	All	Input	82.81	180	54%	140000	778
		Black	Grp A,B	Input	82.81	180	54%	100000	556
	3001	Green	All	Input	82.81	180	54%	190000	1056
		White	All	Input	82.81	180	54%	170000	944
		Grey	Grp A,B	Input	82.81	180	54%	130000	722
Product group 2			Intake units						6944
			Intake selling value					1250000	
			Merchandise intake plan					1250100	
3	1003	Purpl	All	Input	103.42	220	53%	150000	682
		Yellow	All	Input	103.42	220	53%	170000	773
		Orange	Grp A,B	Input	103.42	220	53%	120000	546
	2003	Pink	All	Input	103.42	220	53%	170000	773
		Brown	All	Input	103.42	220	53%	190000	864
		Black	Grp A,B	Input	103.42	220	53%	130000	591
	3002	Green	All	Input	103.42	220	53%	180000	808
		White	All	Input	103.42	220	53%	170000	783
		Grey	Grp A,B	Input	103.42	220	53%	130000	591
Product group 3			Intake units						6411
			Intake selling value					1410000	
			Merchandise intake plan					1410100	

Total Dept XYZ	Intake units		25655
	Intake selling value	4040000	
	Merchandise intake plan	4040700	

Section B represents the the monthly and weekly intake required across time in the same or similar shape as the merchandise intake plan in units per style in units which represent the quantities that will be required to be contracted and reflectected on the production plans of the relevant suppliers.

The total values are summarised in units, intake value and relationship to the financial merchandise intake plan by month and week

Section B

Month 1				Month 2				Month 3			
week 1	week 2	week 3	week 4	week 5	week 6	week 7	week 8	week 9	week 10	week 11	week 12	week 13
150	175	200	225	125	175	200	275	150	200	200	175	250
120	140	160	180	100	140	160	220	120	160	160	140	200
96	112	128	144	80	112	128	176	96	128	128	112	160
72	84	96	108	60	84	96	132	72	96	96	84	120
138	162	185	208	115	162	185	254	138	185	185	162	231
115	135	154	173	96	135	154	212	115	154	154	135	192
46	46	54	61	38	54	61	84	46	61	61	54	77
738	861	981	1107	615	861	981	1353	738	984	984	861	1230
82900	96600	110400	124200	69000	96600	110400	151800	82800	110400	110400	96600	138000
82830	96635	110440	124245	69025	96635	110440	151855	82830	110440	11044	96635	139050
708		125										
567		100										
378		67										
				803		142						
				661		117						
				472		83						
								897		158		
								803		142		
								614		108		
1853		292		1936		342		2314		408		
297500		52500		348500		61500		416500		73500		
297600		52400		348700		61600		416400		73400		
580		102										
657		116										
464		82										
				657		116						
				734		130						
				502		89						
								685		123		
								667		116		
								502		89		
1701		300		1893		335		1854		328		
374220		65000		416500		73500		409000		72000		
374010		65920		416800		73450		409020		72100		
4292	861	1573	1107	4444	861	1658	1353	4906	984	1720		
754520	96600	227900	124200	834000	96600	245400	151800	907300	110400	255900		
754440	96635	228760	124245	834525	96635	245490	151855	907250	110440	156544		

The model assumes the following.

The plan is for a department that has one continuity product group and two product groups for input fashion styles.

The catalogue makes a provision to keep in line with the product and location matrix plan.

The shape of intake across time is regulated as per the shape reflected in the merchandise sales plan.

The period being planned is for three months of a six month season.

The merchandise intake plan row is included for a direct comparison to the merchandise plan intake values for easy reconciliation to ensure that the planned buy is in line with the financial intention.

The intake margin column enables the continual monitor to ensure that the target intake margin is on track with that as deemed to be in the strategy.

The closing stock is determined using the weeks forward cover and therefore takes into account the sales values of the first few weeks in the next phase in order to calculate the closing stocks towards the latter part of the season.

The volumes of the inputs are those that are required to service the catalogue and be on offer for sale until replenished by the next style input. As in the example it is wise to keep a second smaller input to replenish initial sales as some stores will sell out quicker or slower than expected. If the full quantity is put in all at once there could be a situation where there will be pockets of stock left over which will increase the potential of mark downs while on the other hand probable sales will be lost in those stores that are depleted of stock.

The offer for sales time period is determined by the frequency of inputs. In the example above the inputs are the monthly themes and the sales period that are attributed to each style will be for six weeks after which any leftover stocks will be destined for the reduced counters or racks.

Volume and choice balance

The creation of the initial range plan reflects the quantities that have to be bought at item level by colour, in the correct size ranges, at the target mark-ups and retail selling prices. It is essential that the monetary buying amounts of the plan are aligned to the merchandise plan intake values.

The buying plan should reflect the strategy which guarantees the correct amount of selection within the stock parameters while still providing the right spread of products in the required quantities that will best serve the target customer in both style, form and function at any point in time of the season.

During the construction of the plan, the principle that needs to be adhered to is that the merchandise plan must guide the buy with the customer top of mind. Lessons learnt from previous seasons need to be analysed and equally applied to both the basic continuity lines as well as the high end fashion products. Fundamentally it is also important to get the right balance of the correct number of choices in quantities that enable the guarantee of basic lines in depth without impeding the introduction of newness.

It happens often that too much emphasis is placed on the fringe or peripheral lines, or there is excessive similarity in characteristics and price offerings that can disrupt the balance. The emotional wishes of the buying team and suppliers can also have an influence on a distorted balance being achieved and should be guarded against.

The range plan which represents the assortment of products developed within specific categories must represent the organisation of the business and therefore should be balanced across the width and depth of the structure.

The width represents how broad the choice of product is while the depth represents the quantities required to cover the number of sizes and colours including the amount of price points within the product categories. It is probably easier for niche retailers that focus on a narrower customer segment of the market to best be able to serve the both the depth and width demands of their market.

The difficulties that retailers are faced with in striking the right balance of width and depth of ranges is that of presenting real customer choice while at same time optimising the return on investment. In other words, there is the need to attract customers by maintaining a level of newness and fashionability without compromising the traditional or core customers and especially the high volume sellers. It is therefore critical that the buyer has a clear vision of the marketing position and understands the target customer though continuous research which provides the confidence to determine as to what should or should not be kept in the range.

The other challenge of having a too broad choice of styles is that the decision making process becomes an effort to select a product and diminishes the pleasure of the shopping experience.

The volume and choice balance emphasis that the customer expects to find new styles in their size in a variety of colours can be illustrated as follows.

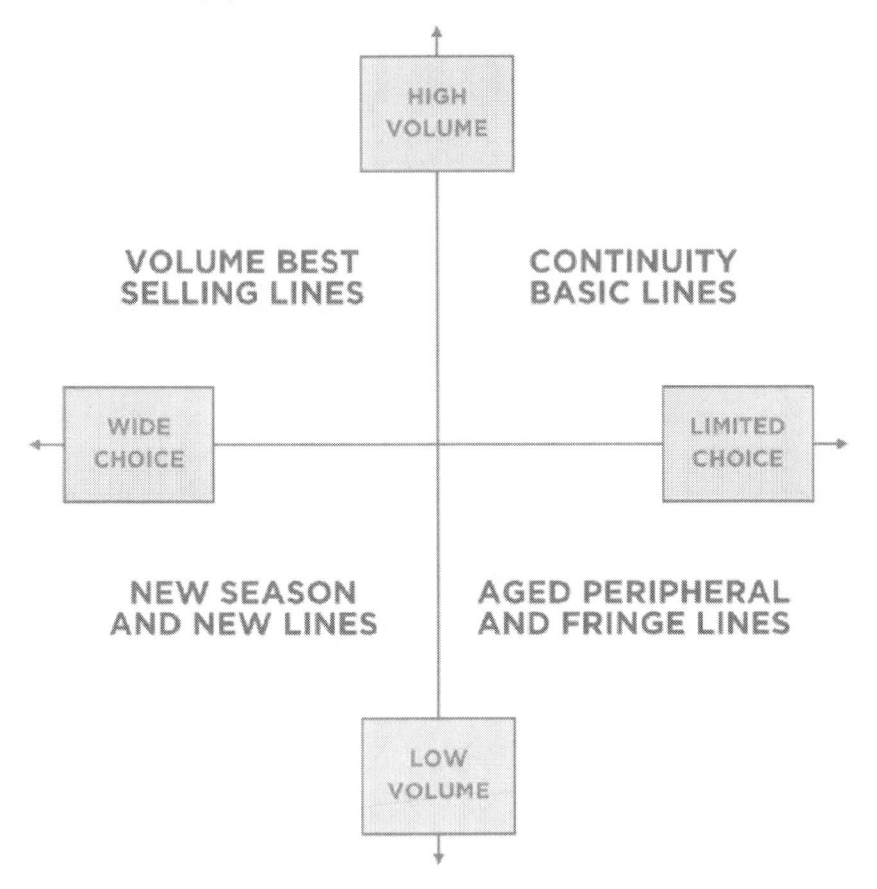

```
                         HIGH
                        VOLUME

        VOLUME BEST           CONTINUITY
       SELLING LINES          BASIC LINES

    WIDE                              LIMITED
   CHOICE ◄─────────────────────────► CHOICE

        NEW SEASON           AGED PERIPHERAL
       AND NEW LINES         AND FRINGE LINES

                          LOW
                        VOLUME
```

Style and shape proportions

The styles that will make up the range structure are dictated by history, the strategy guidelines and direction provided by the design or trend teams.

If one considers the thought process of a customer when a selection is being made, the first feature that she will be attracted to is the style. If the style does not meet the required taste level it will be ignored. The criteria that will influence this choice may not necessarily be the level of fashionability but also the practicality of the garment in meeting the required functionality, examples of which are sleeve lengths, belted or unbelted waists, lengths, neckline or any other feature that will allow the customer to feel comfortable and confident to wear.

Multiple choices form the basis of range plan structure and ensure that all customer preferences are catered for. Another need that has to be provided for is the availability of styling and colours that can be easily coordinated with other product styles within the same or other departments.

Consideration also needs to be given to the cross co-ordination of fashionable items being supported by core product. An example would be a fashion blouse including the core shades in the design or print that would go happily with a basic core skirt in complimentary fabric types. The implementation of this strategy is important as too much deviation from the core pillars will reduce the product relevance and could result in a deterioration of market penetration.

Pricing structure

It is absolutely essential to consider the structure or architecture of pricing across the range in order that a consistent balance is maintained between the good value, mid and luxury price points. Added to this is the controlling of the price movement from one season to the next. The rate of increases or decreases need to be measured on a like for like basis whereby the change in price of identical products is compared to an acceptable overall rate such as the consumer price index while still maintaining the margin targets. Other products should also represent good value in comparison to similar products in the market place.

The philosophy and pricing strategy of the retailer will dictate the balance of price groups dependent on the customer segments that they serve. Probable examples would be where a discount value chain will have about ninety percent of product in the low value band while the middle price type of retailer will have possibly forty percent low price goods with the bulk of products falling into the mid-price range at about fifty five percent. Top end luxury retailers will commonly have in excess of ninety percent of prices falling in the high price range.

A pitfall that needs to be avoided is a scenario where critical price points are maintained through harsh negotiation tactics for more than one or two seasons as it could happen that it will eventually reach a point that without an increase it may become no longer viable for the supplier to manufacture. A decision to then move the price to a realistic level could result in the customer resisting the purchase as a result of the perception that the price is excessive in relation to the previous season. Credibility may also be lost as there may be great difficulty in justifying the narrower gap difference between other products within the range and they in turn could be interpreted to represent poor value.

Extreme deep cut promotions may have a similar impact and the danger exists that the balance of the margins may become distorted. An overall anticipated intake margin is based on planned quantities but in reality is rapidly lessened where repetitive turn-ons of the lower margin product takes place.

A factor that must be considered is the effect of the price movement on unit volumes and whether or not the reduced quantities will still service the store catalogue sufficiently to maintain good continuity. If this is not the case it may require the rationalisation of the number of customer choices offered or a restriction of the store catalogue for the product.

A tactic that retailers frequently resort to in terms of a psychological influence is the selection of the number of price points as well as the pricing terminology. For this reason price points such as 99.00 presents a better perception of value than if the product was marked 100.00. This technique however must be handled with caution as for high ticketed items it is better to present 300.00 rather than 299.00 as this may deliver a message of perceived deviousness. In terms of the gaps between price points, the wider they are among the product groups the better is the value perception. In cases where the customer is bombarded with too many price options it becomes increasingly difficult to assess the value variance between products.

Retailers sometimes apply regional pricing where the income status of customers differ. The result is that customers in the poorer areas enjoy a discount that is subsidised by those in the more affluent areas. Similarly there are unscrupulous retailers who launch a product at an unrealistic high price and after a short period reduce it to a price that delivers a normal margin but is promoted aggressively as great value. These practices once exposed are not well received by consumers and become great topics of discussion on social media.

Colour range

The second determining feature of the product that will influence the purchasing decision will be the colour. Colour is the first element of newness and trend direction that is displayed. Many season's ranges can fail through poor interpretation of the seasonal colour trend. How the colour themes are flowed across the seasons is important as is the harmony that exists with not only the colours within each individual product range but also with the overall look of the store. The visual impact is important in that it transmits a subliminal message to the customer through a fine balance of fashion colours to those that the customer prefers.

Core colours should be banked first even though they may not always be the most exciting. A wise retailer once said "white is a business" and this certainly holds true for black, grey, navy, beige and brown year in and year out. The trending themes such as lilacs, pinks, yellows are more often than not linked to the prevailing trends and will dictate the seasonal themes from month to month. There is a place for the high risk edgy colours such funky pinks, shocking purples and burnt oranges as they provide the theatre even though they may not deliver the best returns.

In order to achieve the best variety it is important to ensure that the planned colour spectrum is reflected as a whole by assigning different colours across the diverse styles in the range with the overall proportions meeting the targets of the strategic intent.

Examining the table below it is evident that the plan is not aligned to the strategic target and therefore a revisit to the proportions will be required to bring them in line with the objective.

NUMBER	COLOUR	UNITS	LY	UNITS PLANNED	TY	TY TARGET
1	White	250	19%	356	25%	28%
2	Black	430	33%	356	25%	25%
3	Stone	130	10%	178	13%	15%
4	Khaki	200	15%	178	13%	12%
5	Red	250	19%	178	13%	10%
6	Pink	40	3%	178	13%	10%
	TOTAL	1 300	100%	1 424	100%	100%

Size architecture

As has been highlighted previously, the first attractor to the customer is the style and then colour but the reality remains that the choice will only be complete if the size is available in the wanted style and colour. For this reason many retailers will display their offerings by size so as to minimize the frustration that results when the size is not available in the desired style and colour.

The need to minimise the non-availability of particular sizes is the main reason as to why special attention should be paid to the careful planning and analysis of size profiles.

It is logical that stores have differing size profiles which are driven by the local demographics, shopping patterns and cultural preferences. For this reason the product groupings and styling features need to be carefully assessed. Typical examples would be that possibly in the rural areas customers may be genetically of a larger stature than their counterparts in the cities and could also have a more conservative attitude than the adventurous city slickers. Religious beliefs may also have an influence where certain parts of the body such as arms need to be covered.

As with the top down and bottom up merchandise planning principle we need to determine the overall national size curve for a department, product category and product in order to place the full combined order with the supplier.

Similarly the accumulated store size profiles have to be derived and aligned with the product size profile in order that allocations can meet both the product and store needs.

The size analysis for small, medium and large emphasis size stores will require differing size ratios for each group.

By way of illustration

The department requires total of 6200 units. Based on historical and trend analysis the target size ratio will represent.

	SMALL	MEDIUM	LARGE	X-LARGE
TOTAL ORDER	1 000	1 500	2 500	1 200
SIZE RATIO %	16%	24%	40%	20%

There are three product styles which may or may not be ordered from the same supplier but each will be in the form of a separate order or contract. Because of the different characteristics of each style, the size ratio requirements may be different.

The quantities in the table below will reflect these separate style orders

STYLE	SMALL	MEDIUM	LARGE	X-LARGE
STYLE A (basic for average customer)	300	500	600	400
% RATIO	17%	28%	33%	22%
STYLE B (larger for fuller figure)	200	600	1 100	800
% RATIO	8%	22%	40%	30%
STYLE C (petite high fashion style)	600	900	400	200
% RATIO	29%	43%	19%	9%
TOTAL	1 100	2 000	2 100	1 400
% RATIO	17%	30%	32%	21%

It is not uncommon in women's sizing designed to fit diverse body shapes to carry different descriptive names. Such variations include the height of a person dependent on the torso or back length, whether the bust, waist and hips are straighter which is usually more relevant to teenagers or curvier for mostly adult women.

Examples of such descriptive categories are commonly misses sizes, junior sizes, women's or plus sizes, petite, junior petite and the like.

In order to cater for the varying size silhouettes of individual stores the relevant size ratios pertaining to the particular stores have to be applied. A practical way of doing this can be done by grouping stores with similar size profiles together and utilise these groupings for planned allocations.

A simple working example is outlined below.

Style A – Basic for average customer

Total units are 1800 units

Assume that the total proportions for the store groupings are

Small size emphasis stores   25%   440 units

Medium size emphasis stores 55%
                                                 990 units

Large size emphasis stores   20%   370 units

Based on historical analysis and trend assessment assume that size % splits across the size range for the various store size profiles will be as follows.

	Small	Medium	Large	X-Large
Small size emphasis stores	22%	27%	32%	19%
Medium size emphasis stores	15%	31%	32%	22%
Large size emphasis stores	13%	21%	37%	29%

The results displayed in the table below reflects in what proportions the total ordered quantity of 1800 will be allocated to meet the size profiles of the individual stores.

	SMALL	MEDIUM	LARGE	X-LARGE
SMALL EMPHASIS STORES	97	119	140	85
SIZE RATIO	22%	27%	32%	19%
MEDIUM EMPHASIS STORES	153	305	320	209
SIZE RATIO	15%	31%	32%	22%
LARGE EMPHASIS STORES	50	76	140	106
SIZE RATIO	13%	21%	37%	29%
TOTAL	300	500	600	379
SIZE RATIO	17%	28%	33%	22%

A typical overall size curve can be illustrated using a Bell type curve

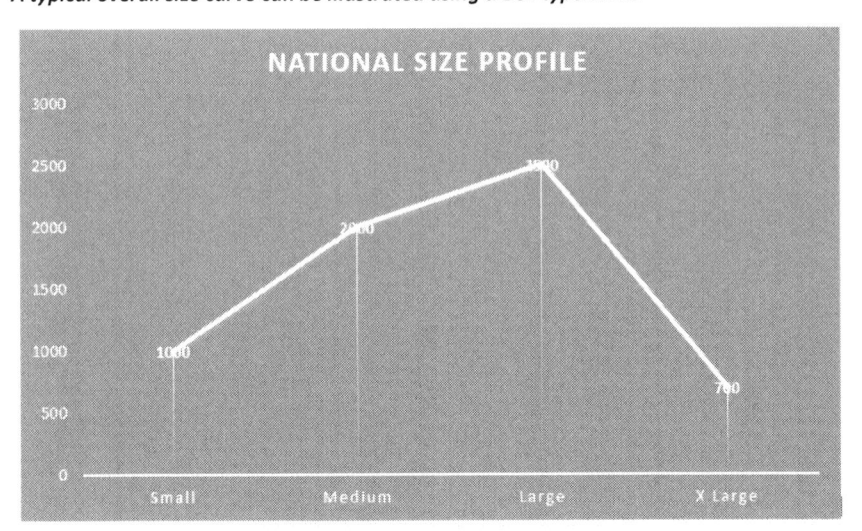

NATIONAL SIZE PROFILE

Size	Value
Small	1000
Medium	2000
Large	2500
X Large	700

While the above represents the overall size curve this will have to be equivalent to the sum of the individual product categories size curves.

For simplicity we can assume that this overall curve is made up of three product types which are a basic type with medium size emphasis, a style for the fuller figure and a high fashion smaller size emphasis requirement. These in turn need to service stores that are size small emphasis, size medium emphasis and size large emphasis profiles.

In conclusion a check list should be drafted which confirms that all the deliverables expected from the range plan are adequately covered. These would include the confirmation of the presence of key looks and trends for the season, that all the end use options are available for the customer, that the range has a look of freshness, the assortment includes the expect to find products and does not contain any duplications.

Validation is required to ensure that the strategic intents of the product group, supplier, sourcing team and designers have been met and lastly that the margin target is achieved.

The use of trials

The trusted use of trial quantities which can be put into stores prior to the season may be intended to test attributes such as styling, colours, prints, fabrics, fashion looks, technical or innovative direction or even a value added feature such as a detachable hood in order to gauge the potential of a market.

The trial must also be specific as to what is being tested and it is not advisable to combine different features at the same time. For example, if the purpose is to test a colour, it should be done in a tried and tested style rather than using a new concept style. If this is not done, it could lead to a confused result as to whether it was the style that was successful or was it because of the colour that sales were disappointing.

In order to get a realistic reading of the potential of an untested product it is important to utilise the stores that represent the target market across the chain rather than simply using the larger stores in an environment where there is all likelihood of selling. It is preferred to use a selected cross section of stores and compare performance against similar control styles in the same stores and then extrapolate the results to all stores in the intended catalogue to determine the overall sales potential of the trial product.

Where open to buy is restricted, which is almost always the case, a recommended tactic is to hive off an amount upfront which will allow the freedom to experiment at any time and potentially grow a high volume line.

Range presentations

It is only natural that before the final go-ahead to commit to production is given that the intended range for the forthcoming season is presented to the senior management of a retail organisation in order to get their views, buy in and sign off as a combined decision making unit.

Prior to the commencement of the season it is normal that the design team briefs management and buying groups of key looks, colour themes and other relevant trends for the forthcoming season, while the post seasonal analysis is presented by the commercial team of the buying groups to highlight some of the key lessons learnt from the previous season's trading. The commercial arm will also get approval of proposed budget levels and strategy intents from senior management to ensure that all are aligned in thinking before going ahead with the planning process and the range build.

The range presentations can take on varying formats but in the main the end objective remains the same in that all stakeholders must be comfortable with the selections and strategies to maximise the sales and profit potential.

The attendees who would participate would normally be senior management and the representatives of the relevant buying teams being the category managers, buyers, merchandisers, technologists, location planners, allocators, marketing team, store representatives, members of the design team and supply chain or logistical team members all of whom may well make contributions where appropriate.

Typical contributions are where the technologists may describe new innovations, the garment technologists or sourcing specialists could discuss supplier issues and describe new suppliers, a store representative will add comment as to possibly the practicality of styling based on what they have gleaned through their interaction with customers, location planners will confirm that the quantities being purchased are sufficient to serve the designated catalogue or will accommodate the volumes required for planned promotions as outlined by marketing.

The agenda is usually commenced with an overall summary by the category manager of the strategy which will refer to supplier sourcing, technological developments, pricing policies, key looks and themes and lessons learnt from the previous year which have been taken on board.

The presentation of the numbers side of the department is done by the merchandiser using the line by line department summary as a point of reference. The main points that are highlighted will be the budget levels emphasising the performance in comparison to last year as well as the proportions of each product category with special attention being given to the splits between the automatic replenishment type product and the more fashionable input lines which will carry the newness and represent the more exciting part of the range.

It is usually with regard to this that some form of clarification may be required where levels tend to deviate from the norm. An example of this may well be reflected in increases that are excessive but are justified possibly by a new initiative or increase in store catalogue that is being introduced. What must be guarded against is that the level of increase of the continuity lines tends to be set more conservatively as the assumption is made that they can grow to a level which will be greater than the budget because the raw material requirement is placed ahead of time. The temptation is thereby to free up funds to enable the introduction or addition of the more fashionable product which will not be as easy to turn on. Technically if thought is applied to this practice, it is nothing else but a disguised form of over buying.

Another point needs to be made with reference to the practice of funding the input fashion lines from the surplus created by the conservative budgeting of continuity lines. If this tactic is employed it will result in the distortion of the buying margin. The reality is that the continuity lines will probably sell at higher levels than budgeted but as they carry more conservative margins the actual overall margin will be less than that which was presented.

Other aspects that will be referred to be the unit increases in relation to last year and comments will be made about the overall increase or decrease in percentage terms and differentiation will be made between the like for like product price movements which should be referenced to the current consumer price index.

The profit margins will be discussed to ensure that the profit objectives are met taking into account the levels of mark downs planned and confirming the reality of these amounts based on historical performance.

The attribute splits need to be confirmed such as short sleeves versus long sleeves, collar versus non collar, tops compared to bottoms, colour ratios, size characteristics, woven versus knitted goods, the fabric type splits and the like.

While the number part of the meeting is often seen as the dull and boring bit with very little exciting exposure to the actual product it nevertheless remains probably the most important part of setting the business end foundation and should be given the attention to detail that is deserved.

Once the numbers have been agreed and all team members are comfortable, the buyer will proceed to present the product that is going to make up the range which is going to deliver the budgetary objectives. The most convenient way is to first display the continuity product that will flow through for the entire season and then drop in the monthly inputs which will emphasise the themes in terms of styling and colour for each relevant month. It is also important to check that the specific looks tie in with the other department's complementary product to ensure themes are aligned.

The products display the detail pertaining to the garment on an attached card such as the quantity being purchased, the catalogue of the stores that they are destined for, the selling price and margin and colours with corresponding swatches. Where possible the product should be in the actual material and make up that will be representative of what will be seen in stores. It may have to be that for product which is earmarked for a latter part of the seasons that CAD boards will have to suffice.

In the presentation of the range by month a recommended tactic would be to build the look by store catalogue where the smaller stores range will be displayed first and ticked off and then followed by what the next band of stores will receive until the full range which the flagship stores will carry is displayed. In this way the range across the full chain can be envisaged and attendees are not misled into thinking that the look of the entire range is going to all stores.

As with other meetings the conclusions should be noted, actions listed with time deadlines attached and an accountability component included. This note should be circulated to all attendees and kept on file to serve as a point of reference should there be disagreement when the actual goods reach the sales floor and they are not remembered as the same that was signed off.

Responsibilities of key presenters at a product and planning review

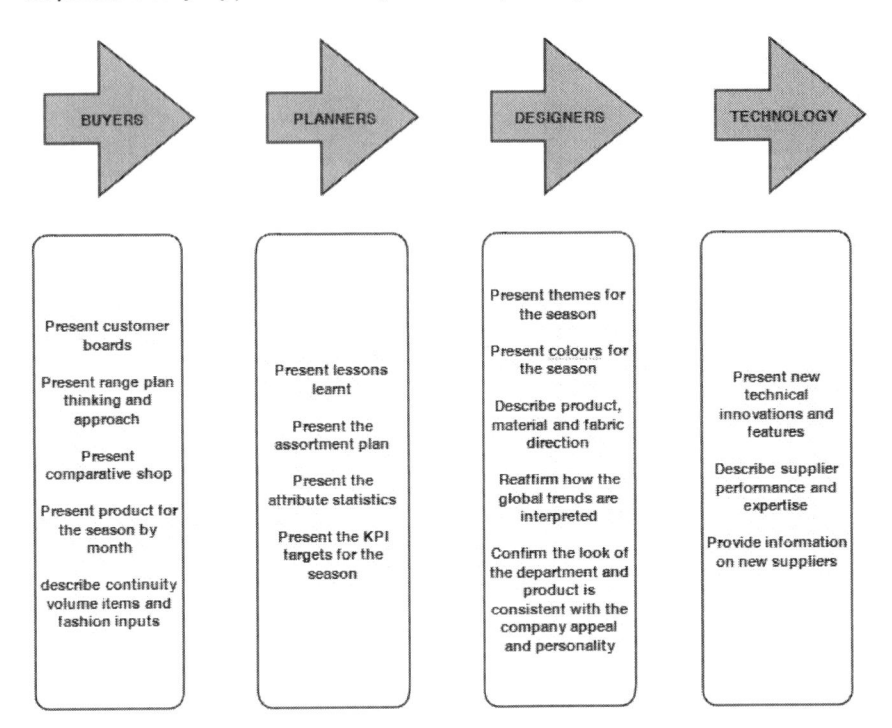

BUYERS	PLANNERS	DESIGNERS	TECHNOLOGY
Present customer boards	Present lessons learnt	Present themes for the season	Present new technical innovations and features
Present range plan thinking and approach	Present the assortment plan	Present colours for the season	Describe supplier performance and expertise
Present comparative shop	Present the attribute statistics	Describe product, material and fabric direction	Provide information on new suppliers
Present product for the season by month	Present the KPI targets for the season	Reaffirm how the global trends are interpreted	
describe continuity volume items and fashion inputs		Confirm the look of the department and product is consistent with the company appeal and personality	

Store range profiling

The differing customer profiles of individual stores is not limited to the size profiles but requires a skilled knowledge of the stores in order that complete customer needs are optimally serviced.

In the main the responsibility rests with the planner while in some organisations there may be dedicated location planners who will study the key attributes of stores in conjunction with the sales and management staff within the stores. This is often a point that is overlooked as it is easy to be too defensive as to the reasons why certain products have not performed to expectation. An objective separate view from those who interact at the coalface with the customer places the reality of the situation in perspective.

Not all stores will be able to stock everything and the catalogues need to flex to best meet the demand for the customer that is served by the particular store.

What is important to note is that the sum of the location plans from individual store to total company need to be in line with the total merchandise plans which are reconciled to the overall buy.

In terms of the forward cover requirements of stores they are dependent on the rate of turnover that the stores enjoy. In principle the high turnover larger stores will tend to have lower forward covers as they need less stock in relation to the volume of sales to maintain effective levels of display whereas at the other end of the scale the smaller low turnover stores which require more stock in relation to their sales to maintain the availability of all sizes and colours all of the time and thus will be replenished less frequently. The typical relationship would be that the larger stores will require in the region of five weeks forward cover whereas the smaller stores may need ten weeks of forward sales to present full availability to the customers. For this reason and the physical constraints it is likely that the smaller stores will carry a lesser number of styles in the catalogue in comparison to the larger units.

The catalogue of the store will be influenced by the demographics, income bands and cultural factors. The process that the location planner will follow when assessing a store is firstly to review the sales levels of the various categories of product and examine those areas where there have been unacceptable levels of markdown and probe the reasons why this has occurred which may result in a decision to remove certain categories. Conversely missed opportunities need to be identified and action plans drafted to ensure that these are optimised going forward.

It is unlikely that the sales shape across time for every store is going to match that of the overall company. A prime example is a coastal resort store will experience seasonal peak sales during holiday periods while will be extremely conservative outside these times or conversely stores will experience depressed sales in university towns where there is an exodus of students during the holiday period.

The frequently recommended approach is to plan each store as if it is your only store. This is however easier said than done particularly where some chain stores may have hundreds of stores. In many cases the control of stocks at micro level can be extremely time consuming and complex but the use of technical software packages have made it possible to accurately measure sales performance and determine stock requirements to the finest detail based on historical sales patterns.

New stores need to be reviewed as the sales shape may be distorted by the initial opening hype or the fact that it may have been only partially open for the period under review. A common approach that is adopted to plan the range selection for new or refurbished stores is to mirror them to a similar profile store and base the quantities on a comparable turnover size store.

Where sales are disappointingly low it might require the de-cataloguing of certain lines or certain sizes of a specific offering in order to minimise markdowns without disappointing a large section of customers and enabling the freeing up of more space to expose good performing ranges more forcefully.

A scenario could exist where stores require a wider assortment of product in lesser quantities. The obvious influencing factors in the main will be space constraints, the changing demographics of the town, the store may have been modernized or a new mall may have opened or closed all of which would justify a wider assortment.

The effective utilisation of space in a store is determined by the percentage sales contribution of each product category. Strategically this may be deviated from, examples of which are where a possible focus is required on a new range launch or because of a younger customer age demographic who have more children will inspire a thrust to aggressively feature children's ranges. In principle these deviations must be carefully considered so that the other product groupings are not placed in danger of being stifled entirely.

The measurement of space is translated into facings or opportunities for the customers to choose from with relevant appropriate values attached for shelves, rails, pegs, table displays in conjunction with the equipment positioning. In other words, a rail in the darkest back corner of the store will carry less value to that on the entry aisle at the front door of the store which enjoys the greatest traffic flow. The placement of total departments will follow the same principle where the highest turnover departments will enjoy the more prominent positioning with greater exposure.

The layout of the store should facilitate a journey through the store from one area to another interlaced with coordinated displays suggesting to the customer options to consider for a complete wardrobe option including apparel, accessories and impulse products before they reach the pay points. Layouts that are static straight up and down rows fail to entice customers to other areas of the store.

STOCK MANAGEMENT

The efficient management of stock is frequently neglected. The inclination is to believe that the more sold, the greater is the profit. While this is true, without the careful management of stock holdings the profit benefit can easily be eradicated. There are a number of reasons for this but it cannot be emphasized enough that constant attention is required to ensure that potential profits are not quickly eroded either through sell outs or overstocks.

The first sign of poor sales of a style is often optimistically justified by assuming that things will get better and the conclusion is too easily arrived at that it is merely a temporary setback. Good examples are thinking that the weather is not quite right, a big event has occupied the customer's minds, and the customer does not understand the product or a competitor had a killer sale at the same time. Inevitably this procrastination of corrective behaviour results in the point of no return being reached and by the time reality sets in, the consequent punishment in the form of higher markdowns could be the result.

Another common trap is that when sales are sluggish to throw more stock at the problem. Store management often justify poor performance by routinely stating that they do not have enough stock. However, upon examination, it is found more often than not that this is not the case and more intense probing needs to be conducted.

Stockholdings must be kept as tight as possible and where essential, the rationalisation through the elimination of fringe sizes and colours or whole ranges from the store catalogue will keep forward covers to a minimum and improve stock turns.

Promotional activity in whatever form that is appropriate can also help to alleviate the situation. Such price cuts or offers must be meaningful and albeit at lower margins, the removal of stock allows the inflow of newer fresh socks together with the freeing up of display area and does not force the banishment of goods to storage possibly never to see the light of day again until the major clearance sales.

Contingency plans should be put in place such as turning off production of slow selling styles, converting the style into more successful shapes and if the problem lies with the colour or fabrication it is better to take the write down on fabric rather than in garment form.

In this day and age where the accuracy of stock data bases is reliant on the efficiency of the information technology systems, the correct labelling of product is absolutely essential so that the precise data is captured which is critical for the effective replenishment of the product.

Pilferage, shop spoilage, customer returns of poor quality products, incorrect stock counts, visual display garments and goodwill donations are part and parcel of the retail environment and such product is rendered unsaleable but remains on the stock records which then distorts the replenishment needs. Stock adjustments are normally done by store staff and as a result the human error factor is very real as well as the manipulation of records is tempting to guarantee a flattering lower shrinkage result.

The more basic continuity lines that are on display for long periods of time are most susceptible to stock inaccuracies. A revealing sign of such a situation may be where stocks are reflected week after week but do not have any corresponding sales on performance documents. The impact of these false positive records is often evident that when sales slowdown of such a style and a new injection of goods with a different stock keeping record suddenly delivers a much improved sales performance.

Some retailers apply a technique of stock ageing where goods are date coded and after a reasonable period of time a particular date code can be considered as phantom or odds and ends and are flushed out by deleting them from the stock record data base.

Fashion input styles may also be date coded and are flagged for price reduction at a point in time when the styles or colours are no longer relevant to the prevailing trends or themes. For this reason the incorporation of date codes in the barcode assists in the correct rotation of stock whereby the older dated stock is sold first but this requires well controlled stock rotation disciplines in warehouses and stores.

The converse situation where the stocks are supposedly non-existent is not as serious as it may still be available for sale. The real impact is dependent on the size of the error as the non-existence of records of stock will attract a need to be replaced and could lead to potential overstocks.

The maintenance of accurate stock data is dependent largely on the well regimented stock takes as in spite of the belief that continual cyclical counts will keep physical stocks in line with theoretical records, the truth is that often these deliver greater inaccuracies as they are not as disciplined and often misplaced stocks, duplicate displays and soiled goods are excluded from counts. Added to this regular stock counts come with extra costs and the value of the product may not warrant the additional effort whereas the more expensive product may well need to be strictly controlled.

Other points where the accuracy of stock records are in jeopardy are at the point where the goods are received. The accurate receipt of product from the supplier at the warehouse needs to be well controlled as if, for example, the goods have the incorrect SKU ticket the receipt will automatically reflect against the wrong product in the scanning process. The withdrawal of stock from warehouse shelves and is subsequently picked and packed for store delivery has to be correctly recorded in order that the balances remain credible.

The receipt by the store is usually done at face value in order that the flow of goods to the sales floor is continuous. This heightens the possibility of pilferage in transit in spite of various preventative security measures. There is also the risk of incorrect documentation or suspect manipulation during the hand over processes.

Where disputes between the stores and the warehouse or distribution centre do arise the settlement of the claim tends to linger on as neither party wish to take on a negative mark against their shrinkage results with the result that final resolution often does not happen.

System errors or incorrect information is very real in the transmission of data between platforms which can go undetected until such stage that the all ills are blamed on "the system" which generates a mistrust which is not easily challenged or disproved but even worse, decisions and adjustments are made using incorrect data.

Supplier meetings
Once the product specification pack is formulated for a particular style, the retailer is in a position to initiate detailed meetings in order to prepare the supplier prior to the commencement of the production process.

It is extremely important that the meetings are well structured, prepared with an agenda, are clear and professional. Most importantly it is critical that the appropriate people are assigned tasks and completion dates are recorded for follow up.

Live information capture using a laptop and projector is very effective as meetings tend to be shorter, decisions and assignments are clear and results can be managed and tracked. The other advantage is that the publication of the minutes is immediate with the action tasks for those accountable being explicitly defined with completion dates.

Negotiating
Negotiation is the process whereby through dialogue between two or more parties an agreement is met and the outcome satisfies the needs of both within the boundaries that the situation will allow.

In the retail environment, negotiations typically revolve around topics such as price, garment content, costs, innovation and profitability. The discussions can take place under high pressure where the expectations of both parties are elevated and the rivalry is intense. Often the relationship may be under threat which may or may not add another dimension depending how significant the association is. The opposite of this can be, and the most suitable, where the two parties collaborate to reach the most desired outcome.

To achieve a situation where both parties benefit, requires maturity, a clear understanding of the end objectives with informed discussions by both parties and the development of a plan to achieve a mutual objective.

Notwithstanding the above the supplier and the retailer will still have their own agendas. The supplier will wish to sell as much as he can for the best price while the retailer will want the product for as cheap as possible for the best quality. If the retailer does not have an insightful understanding of the manufacturing process the chances are that they might end up paying too much or sacrificing content.

Negotiating can be a traumatic experience and not all may have the appetite for the heightened discussion. In the case of the supplier there could be a tendency to avoid the confrontation and at times simply give the product to the retailer for the price requested, while the retailer, on the other hand, will similarly pay the supplier's more expensive proposal without exploring all options to get the best deal.

The retailer must always be well prepared with all relevant facts regarding fabric, trim, ratings and costs, prevailing exchange rate trends, wage structures, margin policies including other external and internal factors at hand in order to be able to have an informed sincere discussion. The persuasion process must be done in a way that the argument is convincing and the acceptance by the other party is seen to be mutually beneficial, trustworthy and incorporates the other participant's needs.

The progression of negotiation follows the steps of preparation, conducting the discussion and reviewing the outcomes.

Thorough preparation is critical which requires that the issues and opportunities are identified, prioritised and have a value for both parties. Focus must be on both the hard subjects such as the monetary issues and volumes as well as the softer matters such as perceptions.

Boundaries must be set in the types of outcome broken up into which would ideally like to be achieved, or what is likely to be achieved and thirdly the bare minimum that would be accepted.

Analysis of the environment of both businesses must be well defined in terms of the markets, competitor activities and the supplier capability and technical expertise required. These factors coupled to the trading history and what percentage the supplier is of the retailer's business and what the retailer represents of the supplier's total production or put differently, who needs who the most.

Past performance and consistency as well as the growth potential and the degree of product uniqueness or cost advantages are important leverage factors that are to be taken into consideration.

Key bargaining points for the retailer are cost prices, discounts, volumes, exclusivity, return policies, promotional support, delivery scheduling and any other unique service while the supplier's focus is likely to be the volumes that can be achieved, the highest cost price that will be agreed and the long term sustainability of regular business.

There is not always a satisfactory resolution to negotiation discussions and contingency plans need to be in place as to what alternatives are available should a deadlock situation be reached. These may include the possibility of moving production to different suppliers, reduce volumes and increasing the levels of other substitution ranges, the consideration of sale or return agreements and although not desirable, possibly increasing the selling price above the norm.

Behaviour and strategies during the meeting are extremely important. Asking for more than is expected will give room for negotiation to what is acceptable without simply accepting the first offer. It is also essential to remain flexible and creative in an effort to avoid a deadlock situation. A vital point to bear in mind is that at all costs to avoid haggling as this practice runs the risk of destroying a relationship.

If confrontation does transpire, it should be tactically done and at all costs does not include any personal attack or involve the use of threats and ultimatums. The power of silence should be remembered as it can be effective and if needs be, try and concede to small bits at a time, park potentially unresolvable issues even if it means that the meeting has to be temporarily adjourned.

There are personal factors that can influence the final negotiation. Different partakers follow different processes, they have diverse experience levels as well as possess varying understandings and personality traits which may be unpredictable.

There is an added complexity in dealing with off shore suppliers where there are duties, logistical challenges, and culture and language differences.

Once the negotiations are concluded, a documented summary of the agreements, commitment of resources, capacity to deliver and action plans is absolutely critical to ensure complete understanding. The record will enable an amicable resolution should any misinterpretation which could possibly become a point of dispute at a later stage.

Costings

It goes without saying that cost forms an integral part of the negotiation process. It is therefore imperative that the retailer has a good understanding of the components and the proportions of a costing sheet thus permitting the ability to test the validity and understanding of any costing presented by a supplier.

The cost of a product is broken down into two distinct categories, namely direct product costs and the costs associated in getting the completed product to the retailer.

Factors that will influence the cost of a product will be the size ratio, which if weighted towards the larger sizes will utilise more fabric or affect the wastage of fabric because of a less efficient marking of the lay of fabric on the cutting table.

The level of detail of the styling may not only affect fabric consumption, it will probably also influence the manufacture time or minute rating.

The width of the fabric can also affect the usage of fabric and the general rule is that the narrower the width of fabric the more expensive the product is likely to be. Specialist fabrics tend to be on narrow width such as 110cm while the full width is 148cm. Woven fabrics can be as wide as 160cm.

Plain or printed fabrics will also affect fabric usage particularly where stripes need to be matched on different components such as sleeve and body and is likely to result in more wastage of fabric.

The components of the cost of the products can be divided into those that are considered to be fixed such as raw materials, overheads which include services such as design, technology and logistics and those that are variable which are in the main the constituents that are squeezed down to meet the demands of the retailer like wages, working hours and production methods.

Packaging costs will also vary for different types of product. The size of the cartons required to transport the product is determined by the dimensions of height and width that must protect and accommodate the garment comfortably. The in store presentation requirements will also affect the overall cost from the point of view that allowance may be needed for hangers as well as additional swing tickets.

Where goods are imported, duties need to be taken into consideration. Duties are normally determined against the free on board value or in other words the cost to place it on the deck of the ship. They can also be calculated as ex works which is the cost as at the completion of production.

Exchange rates are a critical factor. The option to purchase currency ahead of time at a fixed rate to finance the cost provides the peace of mind that the costs will be stable even if the day to day rates fluctuate. If currency is not bought ahead but goods are purchased at the prevailing rates the retailer may be forced to revise selling prices to ensure the achievement of the target margin.

Different categories of products attract different tariff duties at the receiving country depending on country of origin and manufacture as well as protection policies of local production.

The cost to transport the goods from the place of manufacture will vary for local goods or from the port by the clearing agent, depending on the location of the retailer in relation to the supplier or port, the size of the cartons or container and the mode of transport. Included in this section would be freight and warehousing charges.

The typical elements of a product costing and examples of approximate proportions will be

ELEMENT	DEPENDENCY	CATEGORY
TRANSPORT 5%	Different methods of transport used.	Transport / landing 20%
DUTY 30 - 40%	Taxes levied against the import of goods as specified by the local government.	
SUPPLIER MARGIN 10%	Supplier margin can vary between 5% and 15%.	Production costs 80%
WASH AND TRIMS 5%	Costs allocated to special processes or trims.	
PACKAGING 7%	Total cost of all packaging, including presentation.	
LABOUR 28%	The standard minute rates will differ from country to country, depending on operational complexity.	
FABRIC AND MATERIAL 50%	Will be influenced by the garment rating, which will dictate how much fabric is used to manufacture the garment.	

In addition to the product costs as outlined above there are other costs that need to be taken into account in order to get product to market. These can be categorised basically into two categories, firstly being additional costs to the supplier such as the base overhead costs being the total for rent, electricity, administration costs and the like that will always be there and which must be apportioned per product unit.

The second category can be described as being unrelated to the product directly that have to be paid. The main type of such costs are settlement discount agreements, marketing contributions, finance costs and royalties. These together with the product costs will deliver the final cost of the garment.

Points to note in the review of costs are in cases where the supplier throws in vague and unsubstantiated reasons to justify increases. It is essential that the retailer tests such requests to ensure they carry merit.

A typical instance is where the statement is made that wages have gone up and a new costing is proposed. A cross check is required to determine the proportion of what labour represents of the total costing. In the above example this would be the 28% for labour and apply the increase to this part and reconcile to the proposal.

Where increases are attributed to material increases an effort should be made to investigate the trend in the industry and do some comparisons even if they may be a bit crude. If your research shows that the increase is not in line with the trend, the supplier should be encouraged to find a better source and not to pass on the cost of their inefficiencies.

The use of exchange rate fluctuations to motivate cost price changes is more easily resolved as the average movement can be tracked over a period of time and applied. It is a possibility that in fact there might have been an improvement. Foreign currency could also have an influence depending at what price the supplier or retailer may have covered forward.

If the retailer's volumes are increasing significantly the opportunity exists to negotiate a discount in cost price to share the benefits of the improved scale of efficiencies. A point to note is that while this practice is not discouraged, the smaller retailer may not be able to finance the larger volumes of product or growth based incentives. Even with the benefit of a greater margin, the viability remains to be dependent on the organic growth of the chain, for example, the addition of new stores in order to accommodate the higher buying volumes.

A costing approach which is often employed by retailers is that of requesting appropriate suppliers to tender for a product. In order that this is done fairly and equitably the exact same specifications need to be provided to the potential suppliers. Cross costing comparison between suppliers is a popular option where there are large programmes up for grabs and is unlikely to be used for once off high fashion inputs.

For a retailer to commit to high volume programmes, it is a key requisite that the potential suppliers fulfil some basic requirements in that they must be financially stable, have a reliable track record in terms of delivery performance, provide consistent quality with up to date compliancy audits and will be able to cope with the required volumes which could include the agreement to hold a minimum stock holding. The supplier should also be flexible enough to be able to make styling changes to the product where necessary.

The key stipulations for use with cross costing or tenders which will be provided is a detailed style sheet, comprehensive specifications of fabric and trims, the garment measurements with the range of sizes, volumes, a target cost price, packaging requirements and packing methods, delivery dates or production flow.

ORDERING

After the negotiations are completed and the decision to award the production of a style to the supplier is taken, an order has to be drafted to reflect the commitment to the supplier.

The signed order for the supplier is created and placed by the retailer for the entire season in the case of a continuity product or possibly monthly for input styles. It is imperative that it must be done timeously to ensure the required completion date is realistically achievable and the production lead time required will be determined by careful critical path production management.

While the order is in essence a contractual document it will be subject to the overall terms and conditions that are entered into in a memorandum of agreement that is drawn up separately when a manufacturer is appointed as a certified supplier. Production can only commence once the final approved order is in the possession of the supplier.

The contract or the order is the document that details the terms by which the retailer takes ownership of the goods in exchange or payment of an agreed price.

The timing of orders is done according to the range plan guidelines and each supplier will be provided with an extract specific to them for the season. This production programme will indicate the style details, quantities, size ratios and colour specifications which will enable them to plan the production capacity and will be used as the point of reference during follow up production progress meetings. Each style will also have a corresponding style specification sheet which confirm the costs, pack quantities, labels and tickets, wash and care details, testing requirements and the fabric as well as component information.

Orders may be amended where required. These adjustments are normally for quantities, dates, prices and size ratios. The changes need to be recorded on the contract and refer to the date of the alteration as well as the nature of the change.

It is advisable that any style changes require the order to be cancelled and be replaced by a new order as in essence it is a different product.

The order can have two status phases where a pre-production contract enables the supplier to procure fabrics, components, labelling and packaging and make a pre-production or pre shipment sample which will be submitted to the retailer for approval. The sample will serve as the set standard of quality that will be referred to should any disputes evolve in production or in stores.

Production may only commence once a final approved order is received by the supplier.

Documented programmes of continuity lines for the full season may serve as an authorised arrangement from which the supplier will be able to order the raw materials and components but they will only be able to commence production of agreed quantities, for example, for six weekly time periods upon the receipt of an approved contract. This gives the retailer the flexibility to make adjustments based on current performance. Such amendments may take the form of changes to quantities, size ratios and colour quantities.

Dependent on whether the supplier is local or offshore the delivery requirements need to be clearly outlined with all relevant contact details, delivery stipulations, carton markings and delivery addresses.

A typical order for imported and local products will probably be as follows

ORDER								
RETAILER XYZ								
ORDER NO.		DATE						
SUPPLIER		ORDER STATUS	Pre production		Production			
SUPPLIER REFERENCE		COMPLETE/SHIP DATE						
PAYMENT TERMS		LAUNCH DATE						
DELIVERY METHOD		PACK QUANTITY						
DELIVER TO		TOTAL QUANTITY						
		COST VALUE						
		SELLING VALUE						

SKU NUMBER	STYLE NUMBER	STYLE DESCRIPTION	COLOUR	TOTAL COLOUR UNITS	SIZE	TOTAL SIZE UNITS	COST PRICE	SELLING PRICE
100023564	12345	Basic t-shirt	White	1000	S	200	45.00	99.99
100023565					M	400	45.00	99.99
100023566					L	300	50.00	110.00
100023567					XL	100	50.00	110.00
100023568	12345	Basic t-shirt	Black	2000	S	400	45.00	99.99
100023569					M	800	45.00	99.99
100023570					L	600	50.00	110.00
100023571					XL	200	50.00	110.00

BUYER SIGN		MANAGEMENT SIGN					
MERCHANDISER SIGN		SUPPLIER SIGN			DATE		

The information typically included on the order is as follows and will be stored on a data base system for any interested party that needs to access the detail.

Supplier reference number and name

Order number

Date that order was raised

Shipment date and launch dates

Shipping method

Method of payment

Point of delivery

Style number

Style description

Colour break down and quantity

Labelling instructions

Special terms or conditions of trade

SKU number

Size breakdown

Quantities

Number of units per inner pack

Number of inner packs per outer carton

Cost Price less any negotiated discounts

Selling Price

Signatures of authorization to buy are most commonly those of the buyer, merchandiser and a member of senior management. The omission of any of the signatures could result in the order being rendered invalid in the case of a disagreement. A supplier signature is often the rule but the acceptance of the order is in essence the recognition of all the terms and conditions of the order.

It is not uncommon for planning production schedules or provisional orders to be handed over to the supplier prior to the issuing of an official order, particularly in the case of replenishment product where the supplier needs to plan capacity requirements, order raw materials and components but this is by no means the go ahead to commence production. Without the completed signed order no knife may be put to the fabric.

The higher level order may be supplemented by a detailed specification pack and a critical path management document that serves as an appendage to the order and reflect the details and quality references of the fabric and components, sample submission requirements, technical tests, labelling instructions, packaging reference numbers and specifications.

The buying and merchandising team will use the basic information to interrogate orders at any time to check, monitor and if required will amend the orders which may be, for example, quantity or date related. Other areas of operation or parties will also need to have access to orders in order that their activities are completed timeously to safeguard that the final completion date is met.

Technology has to utilise the detail to ensure in the process of managing the critical path that all tests, quality control during the manufacturing process, garment fittings and rail samples are completed timeously.

The finance department need to know all the costing details and terms of payment as well as the proposed selling price to ensure that there is sufficient cash flow available to enable payment and be able to monitor the achievement of the gross profit margins.

The IT departments need to be aware of all orders for the provision of the SKU numbers as well as cater for the generation of the swing tickets or labels that are attached to the garments indicating the style number, colour, size and price detail which are either sent to the suppliers in bulk or the data files are transmitted to those suppliers that have the facilities to generate their own SKU tickets.

The distribution centre must have sight of the orders in the pipeline to assess the size of proposed deliveries going forward to ensure that they are in a position to plan sufficient resources in terms of staffing, equipment, space capacity and that sufficient transport is booked to deliver the goods speedily to stores.

PRODUCT ALLOCATION

Once production is complete the supplier will advise via a report what volumes by size and colour are complete and packaged ready for dispatch to the addresses as stipulated by the retailer.

In a perfect world the intake will match the volumes as indicated on the intake line in the original plan as highlighted earlier.

The intake plan in monetary value was previously planned as follows

	TOTAL SEASON	MONTH 1				MONTH 2				MONTH 3			
		WK 1	WK 2	WK 3	WK 4	WK 5	WK 6	WK 7	WK 8	WK 9	WK 10	WK 11	WK 12	WK 13
OPEN STOCK	77 000	77 000	79 000	82 000	81 000	81 000	88 000	96 000	98 000	98 000	99 000	98 000	91 000	83 000
SALES	370 000	10 000	12 000	14 000	14 000	12 000	13 000	14 000	15 000	13 000	14 000	19 000	21 000	16 000
MARKDOWN	700				700									
INTAKE	376 700	12 000	15 000	13 000	14 700	19 000	21 000	16 000	15 000	14 000	13 000	12 000	13 000	15 000
FWD COVER		6	6	6	6	6	6	6	6	6	6	6	6
CLOSING STOCK	83 000	79 000	82 000	81 000	81 000	88 000	96 000	98 000	98 000	99 000	98 000	91 000	83 000	82 000

	TOTAL SEASON	MONTH 4				MONTH 5				MONTH 6			
		WK 14	WK 15	WK 16	WK 17	WK 18	WK 19	WK 20	WK 21	WK 22	WK 23	WK 24	WK 25	WK 26
OPEN STOCK	77 000	82 000	83 000	84 000	85 000	86 000	87 000	87 000	85 000	83 000	83 000	85 000	85 000	83 000
SALES	370 000	15 000	14 000	13 000	12 000	13 000	15 000	16 000	15 000	14 000	13 000	14 000	15 000	14 000
MARKDOWN	700													
INTAKE	376 700	16 000	15 000	14 000	13 000	14 000	15 000	14 000	13 000	14 000	15 000	14 000	13 000	14 000
FWD COVER		6	6	6	6	6	6	6	6	6	6	6	6	6
CLOSING STOCK	83 000	83 000	84 000	85 000	86 000	87 000	87 000	85 000	83 000	83 000	85 000	85 000	83 000	83 000

Sales will never be exactly as expected as the customers do not have prior knowledge of the plans and will always buy differently. Coupled to this the amount of over or under production due to a reject factor could result in availabilities being higher or lower than what the supplier was meant to make and therefore the actual closing stock at the end of each period will definitely vary to the expectation. Markdown values are also continually different to that planned.

Stocks and sales are the anchor targets that are consistently aimed for with the intake being the balancing variable to bring the plan back in line. In the hypothetical exercise below done for Month 1 of the plan it is illustrated as to how the intake is manipulated over the four weeks of the month in order to meet the original stock targets.

Intake adjustment to reconcile to target stocks

	TOTAL SEASON	MONTH 1			
		WK 1	WK 2	WK 3	WK 4
OPEN STOCK	77 000	77 000	79 000	82 000	81 000
ACTUAL OPEN STOCK	80 000	80 000	80 300	78 800	78 800
SALES	50 000	10 000	12 000	14 000	14 000
ACTUAL SALES	45 600	7 000	10 000	14 500	14 100
MARKDOWN	700				700
ACTUAL MARKDOWN	800			200	600
INTAKE	54 700	12 000	15 000	13 000	14 700
ACTUAL INTAKE	47 400	7 300	8 500	14 700	16 900
FWD COVER		6	6	6	6
ACTUAL FWD COVER		5	5	5	5
CLOSING STOCK	83 000	79 000	82 000	81 000	81 000
ACTUAL CLOSING STOCK	81 000	80 300	78 800	78 800	81 000

To summarise for the month, the total actual monetary value of sales missed target by 4400 and due to the fact that the actual stock opened higher than expectation by 3000 with 100 more markdown then target resulted in the intake for the month having to be reduced from a plan of 54700 to 47400.

It must be noted that the monetary intake requirement needs to be converted to units at the style/colour level to enable the stock availability to be allocated and distributed.

The allocation of product from the availability reports provided by suppliers or stocks stored in the warehouse takes on two methodologies. The input type products, usually for seasonal launches or fashion styles are described as "push" products while the continuity product which is replenished in empathy to sales performance are known as "pull" products where allocations are triggered by minimum stock level points and stopped by the maximum stock level thresholds.

The key differentiators of these types of products are that "push" styles cater for peak sales before being replaced. These styles attract a higher markdown volume as they are removed off display once the range becomes broken as they need to make way for the new themes that the replacement input styles bring.

"Pull" styles determine the requirements based on replacement of actual sales to a pre-determined build to level of stock. The calculation of the quantity of stock required will be the be determined by the amount of intake needed to meet the stock target that is either dynamically determined by the set weeks sales forward cover or is maintained at a static level over time.

"Pull" styles should typically be continuity items that have a predictable rate of sale and have a balanced availability of sufficient volumes of stock from the lowest level to meet the fluctuating demand. The supplier's production planning therefore has to be consistently reliable and flexible to sustain this condition.

The "pull" principle can be illustrated as follows

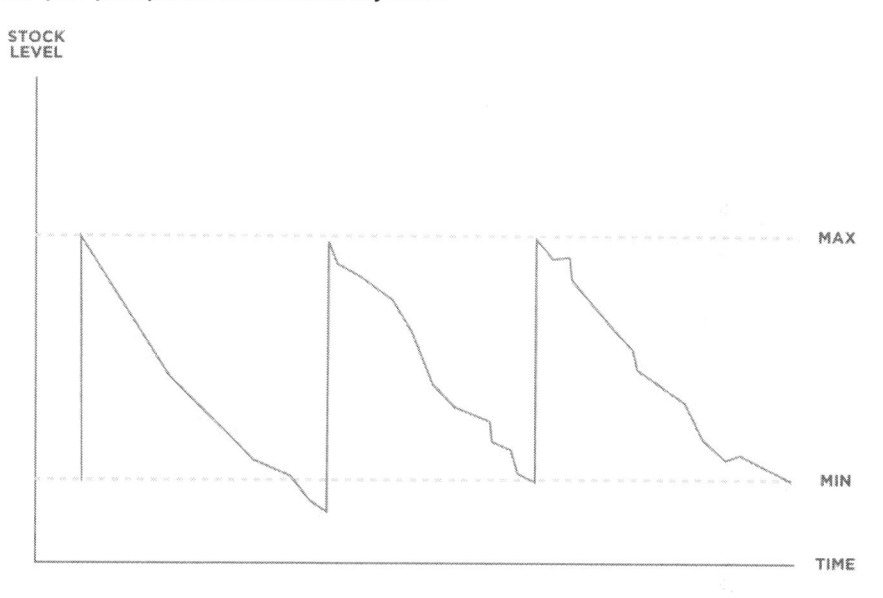

The automatic replenishment or distribution of products is often performed through the use of sophisticated technical allocation systems and are most suitable for the basic continuity product that have consistent predictable sales patterns and for store displays which are laid out according to a centralised space planning system.

The application needs to be merged with the historical sales data and the planned overall sales going forward. In order to achieve a constant replenishment over time a technique of smoothing is utilised where a weighting factor is applied to sales which deviate from the norm due to an unusual event and in such cases the system will use the adjusted realistic level of sale in the algorithm to derive the most appropriate forward allocations.

In the case where there is a launch of new lines, the new line can be linked to the pattern of a similar current style. The performance of the new styles must therefore be very carefully monitored early on and adjusted if need be to ensure the best size provision as possible.

The manual overriding of calculated allocations at store level should only take place in exceptional circumstances for specific reasons such as unforeseen special events, competitor activity or natural disasters. Often the temptation exists to manually override allocations based on an inherent gut feel and this should be avoided at all costs.

The delivery instruction which is sent to the supplier specifies the quantities that must be picked and packed per item per store by colour and size.

The primary size refers to the commonly designated size of all products such as waist measurements, neck and chest sizes while the secondary size refers to products which have other options of the main primary size such as different leg lengths for trousers or varying cup size options in case of bras.

If automated replenishment systems do not exist or are not very sophisticated it may occur that the actual sales by size do not mirror those as planned. In such cases it is necessary to review the size patterns using a manual technique and alter contract ratios going forward. A special balancing contract must be raised for production of those specific sizes that are short in order to realign the size sales pattern to that of the amended regular contracts going forward. A very clear indication where the size ratio is out of line is where at the end of range launches the left over stocks or reduced stocks are dominated by one or two sizes. If one applies one's mind to the consequence of this, it is a fact that potential sales have gone drastically astray of better selling sizes and profit is consequently not maximised.

In summary, the sad part about poor performers or the lack of stock control, is that especially in the case of high volume continuity styles, the resultant negative impact can be likened to a lingering illness that lives with the buying team until the situation of overstocks of unwanted product is eventually rectified or doomed to the reduced counter. It is therefore critical that where there is a hint of such an evolving scenario that very swift action is taken.

Where there has been above average performance of categories, a situation may arise where the amount stock available is unable to satisfy the requirements of the entire store catalogue. In such instances the predicament that exists is one of how to keep everybody happy. The choice usually boils down to reducing the quantities proportionately across the entire catalogue dependent on the priority of need whereby at least each store sees a piece of the pie before sell outs are experienced. The other option is to take the view to shrink the number of stores that are serviced and best satisfy the stores that are more likely to deliver the greatest volume of sales. In many cases it is not uncommon for twenty percent of the catalogue to deliver sixty to seventy percent of the sales. The selection of the second option will retain the credibility of the customers in the bigger units but will disappoint the many customers across the balance of the stores. A tactic to alleviate severe situations is by choosing a geographical cross section of stores and if an on-line facility exists, to ensure that stock is available at all times that can be ordered via the internet.

The use of digital imaging has helped develop realistic three dimensional representations which enable the product to be placed efficiently on the various types of equipment in the store. Such systems operate at detail size level so in theory a store will never be out of a size as the principle applied is that as the store sells one it gets one. The key to the success of such a system is that the data integrity has to be as accurate as possible. If this is not the case, for example, where the data base is distorted through incorrect barcode ticketing or pilferage will result in allocations being calculated inaccurately. The only means to rectify the data base is to do a disciplined full manual stock count from time to time and update the data base accordingly.

Delivery Instruction note example

ORDER NO	12345	DEPARTMENT			Men's Trousers			
SUPPLIER	ABC Manufacturer	STYLE NO			5554			
DATE	14 March, 2015	DESCRIPTION			Casual cotton trouser			

STORES		COLOUR	GREY					
		PRIMARY SIZE	32	34	36	38	40	42
		SECONDARY SIZE	32	34	36	38	40	42
NO	STORE	TOTAL	120	170	160	140	110	100
141	City Centre	250	38	53	50	44	34	66
145	Main Street	200	30	43	40	35	28	53
148	Back Street	250	38	53	50	44	34	66
151	Country Lane	100	15	21	20	18	14	26

REVIEW AND ACTION OPTIONS OF IN SEASON TRADING

Process of comparing the actual performance in relation to the plan

No matter how much time and thought is spent in drafting the strategy and planning forecast it is inevitable that the reality will deviate from what is expected as a result of the volatile internal and external factors that exist at the time. Therefore it is critical to continually review actual performance, analyse the trends and take appropriate action to minimise the risks. Where adjustments are not able to be made to remedy a situation the lessons learnt must be taken on board and banked to be avoided in future trading seasons.

The path to follow in the process of comparing the actual performance in relation to the plan can be outlined as follows

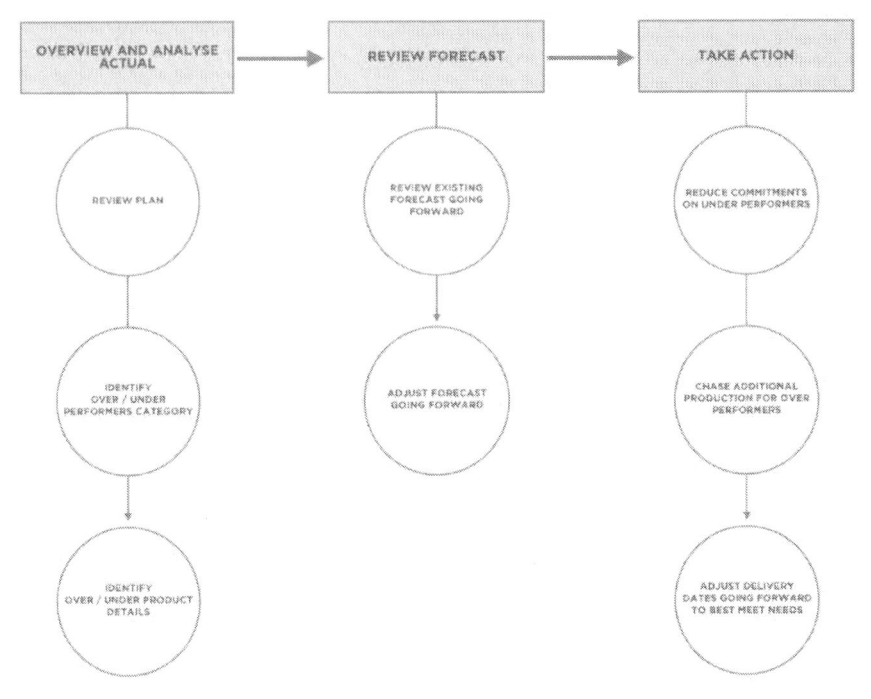

```
┌─────────────────────┐      ┌─────────────────────┐      ┌─────────────────────┐
│ OVERVIEW AND ANALYSE│ ───▶ │   REVIEW FORECAST   │ ───▶ │     TAKE ACTION     │
│       ACTUAL        │      │                     │      │                     │
└─────────────────────┘      └─────────────────────┘      └─────────────────────┘
           │                            │                            │
           ▼                            ▼                            ▼
      ( REVIEW PLAN )        ( REVIEW EXISTING          ( REDUCE COMMITMENTS
                               FORECAST GOING             ON UNDER PERFORMERS )
                               FORWARD )
           │                            │                            │
           ▼                            ▼                            ▼
      ( IDENTIFY                ( ADJUST FORECAST        ( CHASE ADDITIONAL
        OVER / UNDER              GOING FORWARD )          PRODUCTION FOR OVER
        PERFORMERS CATEGORY )                              PERFORMERS )
           │                                                         │
           ▼                                                         ▼
      ( IDENTIFY                                          ( ADJUST DELIVERY
        OVER / UNDER PRODUCT                                DATES GOING FORWARD
        DETAILS )                                           TO BEST MEET NEEDS )
```

The start point of analysing and comparing the actual performance to the intended plan at a point in time, is to firstly to compare actual sales to date at total departmental level and drill down to product level and based on the result, review the planned sales for the balance of the season.

The potential new sales forecast is then compared to the actual commitment of product in the form of stock on hand at stores, product in transit and that at the supplier as well as the orders in the pipeline to determine the resultant shortage or surplus of stock.

In the scenarios below the assumption is that the department consists of a product which is over performing, another that is under performing and one that is selling to expectation.

The procedure which needs to be followed can be broken down into three distinct activities.

- The recording of the total plan for the season in terms of sales and the planned breaking stocks at the end of the season as well as the current week's performance which has just been completed.

- Based on the comparison of the actual sales to date in relation to that which was budgeted for may require a review of the balance of sales to be achieved and thereby create a revised forecast for the total season. The change in the sales forecast may

also then require an adaptation of the planned breaking stocks to reflect the reality of the sales plan.
- Once the realistic revised sales performance has been established, the result then needs to be compared to the total stock commitment and assessed whether there is sufficient stock in the pipeline to achieve the revised targets. If this is not the case, a plan has to be devised in order to determine what action is required to achieve this or conversely there may be a consequent surplus of stock which will have to be reduced.

Analysis and adjustment of sales and commitment status tabulated in three focus areas

TOTAL SEASON STATUS AND CURRENT SALES

STYLE NO	DESCRIPTION	SELLING PRICE	LY SALES	SEASON BUDGET	% INC / DEC ON LY	REVISED SEASON F/CAST	% INC / DEC ON LY	BUDGET CLOSING STOCK	REVISED CLOSING STOCK	WEEKS LY ACTUAL SALES	WEEKS SALES BUDGET	WEEKS ACTUAL SALES	% INC / DEC ON LY
1234	Round neck t-shirt	99.99	950 000	1 100 500	15.8%	1 016 500	7.0%	180 000	150 000	35 000	42 300	39 000	11.4%
1235	V-neck t-shirt	120.99	990 000	1 150 100	16.2%	1 260 000	27.3%	250 000	200 000	38 000	43 700	45 000	18.4%
1236	Button down t-shirt	150	1 100 000	1 200 000	9.1%	1 210 000	10.0%	220 000	220 000	38 000	41 100	41 000	7.9%
	TOTAL DEPARTMENT		3 040 000	3 450 600	13.5%	3 486 500	14.7%	650 000	570 000	111 000	127 100	125 000	12.6%

PROGRESSIVE SALES STATUS

			6 WEEKS TO DATE						20 WEEKS BALANCE TO ACHIEVE				
STYLE NO	DESCRIPTION	SELLING PRICE	PROGRESS LY SALES TO DATE	PROGRESS BUDGET SALES TO DATE	% INC / DEC ON LY	ACTUAL PROGRESS SALES TO DATE	% INC / DEC ON LY	PROGRESS REVISED SALES TO DATE	% INC / DEC ON LY	BALANCE OF LY SALES	BALANCE OF BUDGET SALES TO ACHIEVE	% INC / DEC ON LY	REVISED BALANCE OF SALES TO ACHIEVE	% INC / DEC ON LY
1234	Round neck t-shirt	99.99	190 000	220 000	15.8%	205 000	7.9%	210 000	10.5%	760 000	880 500	15.9%	811 500	6.8%
1235	V-neck t-shirt	120.99	250 000	290 500	16.2%	318 000	27.2%	300 000	20.0%	740 000	859 600	16.2%	942 000	27.3%
1236	Button down t-shirt	150	235 000	250 505	6.6%	252 000	7.2%	252 000	7.2%	865 000	949 495	9.8%	958 000	10.8%
	TOTAL DEPARTMENT		675 000	761 005	12.7%	775 000	14.8%	762 000	12.9%	2 365 000	2 689 595	127 100	2 711 500	14.7%

COMMITMENT STATUS

			COMMITMENT SELLING VALUE					OVER / UNDER STATUS				
STYLE NO	DESCRIPTION	SELLING PRICE	STORE STOCK	TRANSIT STOCK	SUPPLIER STOCK	SUPPLIER OUTSTAND. ORDERS	TOTAL STOCK COMMIT	REVISED SALES BALANCE	REVISED CLOSING STOCK	TOTAL BALANCE OF SALES & STOCK	TOTAL OVER / UNDER SELL VALUE	TOTAL OVER / UNDER UNITS
1234	Round neck t-shirt	99.99	250 000	100 000	280 000	500 000	1 130 000	811 500	150 000	961 500	168 500	1685
1235	V-neck t-shirt	120.99	280 000	70 000	200 000	400 000	950 000	942 000	200 000	1 142 000	-192 000	-1587
1236	Button down t-shirt	150	250 000	100 000	120 000	700 000	1 170 000	958 000	220 000	1 178 000	-8 000	-53
	TOTAL DEPARTMENT		780 000	270 000	600 000	1 600 000	3 250 000	2 711 500	570 000	3 281 500	-31 500	45

Logically speaking based on the tabular representation above of the scenarios, the thought process may well progress as follows.

Scenario 1: Style 1234 round neck t-shirt selling for 99.99 currently has an original season's budget of 1,100,500 which represents a 15.8% increase on last year. Based on the actual performance during the past six weeks the budget is set at a value of 220,000 that still represents a 15.8% where in fact the actual 6 weeks have performed to a value of 205,000 which is only 7.9%. Based on this fact the reviewer then thinks that going forward for the balance of the season a potential increase of 6.8% is more probable than the 15.9% originally planned. Adjustment to the revised level will result the total season being 1,016,500 rather than the 1,100,500 originally anticipated. At the same time the view on the breaking stock is that it will be 150,000 based on the reduced sales for the balance of the season rather than the original plan of 180,000. Thus the stock requirement to complete the sales to the end of the season as well as meet the revised closing stock need means the amount of stock necessary is 961,500. However, when the actual stock in stores, stock in transit, and stock at the supplier as well as outstanding orders still planned to be produced totals 1,130,000 it is clear to see that there is a surplus of 168,500 which at a selling price of 99.99 translates into 1685 units. Action is required to deal with this over commitment. Options are described later on in this section.

Scenario 2: Style 1235 v neck t-shirt selling for 120.99 currently has an original season's budget of 1,150,100 which represents a 16.2% increase on last year. Based on the actual performance during the past six weeks there have been revisions to a value of 300,000 that represents a good 20.0%, however the actual 6 weeks have over performed to a value of 318,000 which is 27.2%. The reviewer then thinks that going forward for the balance of the season an increase of 27.3% is therefore more probable than the 16.2% originally planned which will result in the total season being 1,260,000 rather than the 1,150,100 originally anticipated. At the same time the view on the breaking stock is that it will be 200,000 based on the higher sales going forward will erode stocks and will be less than the original plan of 250,000. The stock requirement to complete the sales to the end of the season and to meet the revised closing stock need means the amount of stock required is 1,142,000. However when the actual stock in stores, stock in transit, and stock at the supplier as well as outstanding orders still planned to be produced it is clear to see that there is a shortfall of 192,000 which at a selling price of 120.99 translates into a deficit of 1587 units. Action is required to deal with this under commitment.

Scenario 3: Style 1236 Button down t-shirt. In this scenario the same process as followed in scenarios 1 and 2 delivers the result that the style performed closely to what was planned and was only 53 units short of target which therefore resulted in no need for any action.

Analysis options
Before deciding on what action is required there are consistent questions that need to be answered. In terms of why the sales differ to the plan one needs to determine whether the sales were early or late possibly due to seasonal factors or extraordinary events. However if they are low the question must be asked whether it is because the appeal to the customer is below expectation.

Measurement against key targets should also be considered as well as the guidelines that are outlined in the strategy. The proportions of the customer segmentation may be incorrectly projected. The pricing policy such as price tiering could be incorrectly balanced, new initiatives may be over optimistic or colour trends are not be as expected and therefore the deviation should be examined down to the lowest level of the hierarchy.

Key performance measures to focus on are forward cover targets to confirm that they are in line or if they are too low the reason may be that there is not enough stock in the system to enable achievement of targeted sales. The measures at store level need to be evaluated as the bigger selling stores may be significantly impacting sales if their individual targets are not being achieved.

Sell off percentage which is defined as the total stock received divided by sales expressed as a percentage, is often used as a key measure but a word of caution is that this needs to carefully assessed as sales with low stocks may deliver a flattering result that leaves a lot better impression than deserved or conversely a disappointing sell off percentage of a product may be due to a full delivery having been received in the latter part of the period and therefore the opportunity to sell was restricted. The value that this measurement has is only truly valid when all products being measured are for the same period of time when full stocks were in place and then can be used as a fair relativity measure between products or to the comparable acceptable levels of sell off.

It is key that all planned promotions and deliveries are still in line to be launched as scheduled and that there are no risks of late or non-delivery from the supplier as this will impact on performance for the balance of the season.

Historical comparison must be considered carefully especially in the case where events fall differently in that this year they may fall on the weekend instead of a week day as may have been the case in the previous year. Special events unique to the season could also have a significant effect. Much of this type of insight is gained through regular store and supplier visits, as well as strict adherence to meeting schedules that include all of the stakeholders comprising of buyers, merchandisers, allocators, designers and technologists. Working as a team keeps everyone involved and committed to an action plan complete with assignments and timelines and a system of updates that monitor the progress of action items.

Differing trends or patterns to that expected may have evolved such as prints which may emerge to be in higher demand than plains.

The review of better selling products as well as the worst sellers needs to be analytically done in an attempt to understand as to why they are performing as they are. Factors that may be common are styling features, colourations, functionality or fabrications. Styles programmed going forward should be reviewed for the identification of opportunities to adapt or change, move out or pull forward and if possible turn on or cancel production.

Regular probes on the sales floor and interaction with sales staff and customers often reveal obvious reasons which are commonly overlooked particularly when one is, as is typical, too close to the detail. Customer focus groups can also provide valuable comprehensions into the practical needs of the consumers and highlight opportunities where sales can be improved and poor quality issues may be exposed.

Action options
In scenario 1 the various possibilities should be considered where action is needed to reduce the commitment in order to minimise potential markdowns.

The stage of completion of the outstanding orders must be determined and if the fabric has yet to be cut, an immediate hold should be put on the order. It is preferable to be left with uncut fabric than with made up garments. The fabric can possibly be converted into other areas of need and be made up in faster selling styles if it is appropriate. Fabric can be held over to be incorporated into a future season's programme if suitable but if it is not right, the last resort would be to sell the fabric off and take the loss on the fabric alone.

Outstanding orders or made up goods at suppliers may need, where possible, to move out the delivery dates or alternatively cancel unmade orders. A point to note is that this decision may require sensitive negotiations with the supplier's in order that they fully understand reasoning and it is encouraged that the resolution of the situation becomes a collaboration of problem solving.

The sales performance at individual store level should be carefully analysed and where there are stores that are selling the product at acceptable levels, that stock is moved from underperforming stores to those where there is a likelihood of improved sell offs. When this is considered as an option it is important to weigh up the cost of the relocation of the product against the possibility of clearing the goods at an acceptable rate. If it is deemed not to be workable it should not be done. Where the product is not in all stores, the temptation is often to extend the catalogue in the hope that the goods may be cleared through greater exposure. This may, however simply spread the problem so should be contemplated with great caution.

A successful strategy could possibly be to launch a promotion and sell the goods at a discounted price in whatever form. The practice may be a simple price reduction, a "two for one" campaign or special discount offers to loyalty programme members.

If all else fails, the last resort is to remove the product from display as it is possibly clogging saleable space and hold back from allocating any stock at the supplier and wait for the major seasonal sale launch to clear the goods. What is essential is that it needs to be clearly understood as to why the product was not wanted and bank the lessons for future seasons to ensure the errors are not repeated.

In the scenario 2 the net result showed that there was a shortfall of required stock due to over performance and the action required would enable the maximisation of the opportunities to achieve additional sales.

The first investigation that should take place is to see whether additional product can be turned on which is dependent on the availability of fabric, components and production capacity. The possibility of converting slower selling styles planned for the balance of the season is frequently a feasible option. Any existing outstanding orders should be pulled forward and the gap that evolves be replaced with the turn on orders. A word of warning is that while the temptation exists to turn on product it is critical that the delivery timeline will allow the full achievement of potential additional sales. If the delivery is too close to the end of the trading period particularly in the case of seasonal product it may result in the product landing up on the reduced counter and thereby eradicating the benefit of extra profits.

The analysis of sales at store level may reveal that certain stores are underperforming in relation to other stores and therefore the catalogue could be reduced to ensure continuity of stock in those stores that are delivering above average sales.

In the same light as the identification of the unique feature of the underperforming product, it is equally important to understand the features that can be attributed to the good performance of other products and put on file for future referral.

POST SEASON TRADE ANALYSIS

A key focus in the assessment of the past performance for the season is to compare the actual key numbers to that what was expected and understand the deviations whether they were positive or negative. The learnings are imperative in the compilation of a new season's strategy and setting of targets.

The key topics that need to be questioned and evaluated are:

Product
- Were the trends which were anticipated in line with what actually materialised? What needs to be taken into account when predicting the future season's trends?
- Did the strategy that was set for the brand and customer together with that of the group and department as well as the supplier selection deliver the envisaged objectives? What needs to be done differently for the new season?

Customers and competitors
- Did the information on customer segmentation and the action plans cater effectively in the satisfaction of the needs? What adaptations and additional resources are needed for the future season?
- Did the competitor initiatives which were anticipated actually happen and was it possible to effectively counteract them? What other methodologies are available to keep up to date with the market place activities?

Key performance Indicators
- Were the targets of sales, margins, stock levels and turns, gross and net profits achieved as per plan or were they unrealistic? What measures require review and which activities are needed to be put in place to achieve them in the new season?
- Was the product assortment in the right proportions and did they perform to acceptable levels to cater for all customer segments effectively? Were the product innovations and promotions that were implemented successful and at the right levels?
- What were the actual colours and sizes sold in comparison to the volumes purchased and what should have been bought instead?
- Identify product sales which need to be adjusted to a realistic level as a result of product failure, poor availabilities and any other factors such as competitive activity

and what special events were there that may have influenced sales either positively or negatively.

Suppliers
- Did the suppliers perform to the levels that maximised availability in the right quantities and on time?
- Did the selected suppliers possess the right capabilities to deliver the programmes that were allotted in terms of innovation, complexity, capacity, quality and on time delivery? Are there other suppliers who should be considered?
- Was the feedback received from suppliers of a nature that can help improve the working relationships going forward?

Stores
- Were stores able to understand the structure of the ranges and easily display them to emphasize the thinking of the buying team? What improvements to guidelines can be made to assist them?
- Was the feedback received from stores valuable and what mechanisms can be implemented to improve the quality of feedback?

Marketing
- Were the marketing channels that were utilised effective and was the uplift in sales able to be measured accurately against control products? Which other communication mediums would be considered?
- Were the promotions successful and what was the extent of substitution purchases?
- What was the feedback from store staff and customers?
- Were the social initiative objectives achieved?

CONCLUSION

There are some significant messages that the reader can be left with after reading through this book. Without doubt, although the emphasis on planning the financial aspects may look cumbersome and tedious to some it is nevertheless the foundation of ensuring the maximisation of profits through accurate preparation.

The construction of a well balanced range of merchandise within the budgetary parameters that has both a broad exciting and innovative selection of merchandise that serves all stores with depth and continuity is absolutely crucial to fully satisfy the needs of the consumer in order to capture the highest market share advantage over competitors.

It is only with continual review of the actual performance and reference to the planned strategy and targets coupled with detailed analysis and swift corrective action that the achievement of the expected key performance indicators can be safeguarded.

It is true that not all expectations will be fully met or opportunities will be missed. These instances need to fully understood in terms of as what the lessons are that need to be banked and heeded in the preparation of the season ahead.

The successful process of understanding the arithmetic of retail, merchandise assortment planning and trading is underpinned by the common phrase "retail is detail".